D1009743

RISKING FAITH

DR. STEVE STEPHENS

A 40-Day Journey

into the Mystery

of God

Tyndale House Publishers, Inc.

Carol Stream, Illinois

Visit Tyndale's exciting Web site at www.tyndale.com

TYNDALE and Tyndale's quill logo are registered trademarks of Tyndale House Publishers, Inc.

Risking Faith: A Forty-Day Journey into the Mystery of God

Copyright © 2008 by Dr. Steve Stephens. All rights reserved.

Cover photo copyright © by Image Bank/Getty Images. All rights reserved.

Author photo copyright © 2007 by Steve Liday Photography. All rights reserved.

Designed by Jessie McGrath

Unless otherwise indicated, all Scripture quotations are taken from the *Holy Bible,* New Living Translation, copyright © 1996, 2004. Used by permission of Tyndale House Publishers, Inc., Carol Stream, Illinois 60188. All rights reserved.

Scripture quotations marked NIV are taken from the HOLY BIBLE, NEW INTERNATIONAL VERSION®. NIV®. Copyright © 1973, 1978, 1984 by International Bible Society. Used by permission of Zondervan. All rights reserved.

Scripture quotations marked AMP are taken from the *Amplified Bible®*, copyright © 1954, 1958, 1962, 1964, 1965, 1987 by The Lockman Foundation. Used by permission.

Scripture quotations marked NKJV are taken from the New King James Version®. Copyright © 1982 by Thomas Nelson, Inc. Used by permission. All rights reserved. *NKJV* is a trademark of Thomas Nelson, Inc.

Scripture quotations marked KJV are taken from the *Holy Bible*, King James Version.

Library of Congress Cataloging-in-Publication Data

Stephens, Steve.
  Risking faith : a 40-day journey into the mystery of God / Steve Stephens.
    p. cm.
  Includes bibliographical references.
  ISBN-13: 978-1-4143-0600-1 (sc : alk. paper)
  ISBN-10: 1-4143-0600-8 (sc : alk. paper)   1. Spirituality. I. Title.
  BV4501.3.S746 2008
  248.4—dc22   2007033322

Printed in the United States of America

14 13 12 11 10 09 08
7   6   5   4   3   2   1

DEDICATION: | **TO ALL THOSE MEN AND WOMEN WHO HAVE BRAVELY GONE BEFORE, SETTING A SHINING EXAMPLE OF WHAT RISKING FAITH IS ALL ABOUT.**

TABLE OF CONTENTS

WELCOME HARDSHIP

PLUNGE DEEPLY

GIVE BACK

I was a reluctant Christian.

When I was six I felt as though God tricked me into accepting Jesus into my heart. I was so mad, I swore just like Uncle Harry. My uncle Harry used to swear at people who talked about anything Christian. He had been raised as a strict Seventh-Day Adventist, and something had happened when he was a teenager that made him hate Christians. If anybody asked him about it, he would just swear. I liked Uncle Harry. He had cool tattoos and rolled his own cigarettes. I might not have agreed with Uncle Harry, but he was always honest and you knew where he stood. I never told him I liked to pray, read my Bible, and go to church. I was afraid he'd swear at me.

I can't imagine a life without God. He gives everything meaning and hope and excitement. Uncle Harry made me sad because after he had his first heart attack he got real scared of dying. Since he believed this world is all there is, he didn't have any hope. When he had his second heart attack he died.

Uncle Harry wasn't a Christian, but there were certain things he believed in that I agreed with. After all, a lot of Christians embarrass me; some just tick me off. Yet this doesn't mean there aren't rational and compassionate Christians in the world. There are just a lot of the obnoxious kind, and they seem to get the most press.

I once had a pastor who said, "Don't let my bad example keep you from a good God." I liked Pastor Fischer. He was kind and listened a lot and loved everybody. Uncle Harry would have liked him. Pastor Fischer would have put his arm around Uncle Harry and said, "Don't be afraid. God loves you." Uncle Harry would have sworn a whole lot, but that wouldn't have stopped Pastor Fischer.

Even as a young child I knew that God loved me, but I didn't want to be a Christian. I wanted to please God, but Christians and churches freaked me out. So I made a deal with God. I told him that if he would only give me a "five-minute warning" before I was going to die, I would gladly accept him into my heart. In the meantime I would do my best to say my prayers, obey my parents, and not smoke cool, hand-rolled cigarettes like Uncle Harry. I thought God and I had a pretty good deal. I kept my end of the deal, and I thought he would do the same.

About a year later I awoke suddenly in the middle of the night and sat up in terror. I heard a large plane bearing down on our house. It got louder and closer. The noise was deafening. Soon this plane would crash into my bedroom and it would all be over. God was giving me my "five-minute warning." I quickly slipped out from under my covers, knelt beside my bed, and asked Jesus to forgive my sins. Then I crawled back into bed and waited for the crash.

At that moment the plane flew over my house and faded into the distance. I was alive and I was so mad. On top of that, I was a Christian and I was stuck. It took me a year to forgive God for that one.

Sometimes I still feel uncomfortable with the word *Christian*. It was once an enlightened word, representing something deep and noble and extremely good. But lately it has become terribly tainted.

It's sad that when people think about Christians, they don't think positive things. In fact, they often think just the opposite.

Over the years I have tried to be a different type of Christian from those I saw around me as a child. I decided I wouldn't follow the status quo of the ordinary Christian. I would chart my own course, taking nothing for granted. I would ask a thousand questions, with only my Bible as my compass and my heart as my guide. I have made a lot of mistakes, taken many wrong turns, sinned, said stupid things, hurt others, been judgmental, been hypocritical, been selfish, been dishonest, had a bad attitude, and done a hundred other things that weren't very healthy. Through it all, however, I've loved God and tried to walk with him. On my journey, I've attempted to follow Jesus, not churches or clichés or theologies or popular authors—every one of which disappoints me. Jesus has never disappointed me.

Join me on this fascinating and exciting adventure of faith. Please don't follow me, for I will surely let you down. I used to have a lot of great answers, but many of them now sound hollow. Yet this is not a bad thing. In fact, it's wonderful. For in place of my cut-and-dried, follow-the-numbers, basically boring faith, I currently see glimpses of glory, which blind and baffle me but leave me energized and desperately yearning for more. So please join me as a fellow traveler and walk beside me as we . . .

+ look at God's creation
+ listen for God's voice
+ study God's Word
+ feel God's heartbeat
+ celebrate God's goodness
+ embrace God's lessons

+ wonder at God's mysteries
+ accept God's ways
+ dance with God's grace
+ love with God's passion

This journey of risking faith is not easy or predictable. If you come with expectations, you will be disappointed. It is full of twists and turns. You never know for sure what is around the next corner. On some days you will laugh with a freedom you never thought possible. On other days you will stand in mind-stretching awe as you peek over the edge of infinity. This journey is not for the faint of heart or for rigid conformists. It is only for those who dream of another world with a provocative, exciting, soul-shaking, absolutely real, passionate, mysterious faith.

This journey to discover the interaction of the physical and spiritual universe is amazing. The journey may also be challenging and lonely, but you will not be alone. Teresa of Avila wrote, "The feeling remains that God is on the journey too." Teresa of Avila is correct: God is with us. Yet we must step out in faith, for he is not always obvious. Sometimes he is a mere sparkle of light or a whisper on the wind or a tug of the heart. God will always defy expectation and explanation, but he will always be there. So step out and risk, and let the adventure begin.

01 | SAIL BEYOND

"The Christian faith is the most exciting drama that ever staggered the imagination.
—DOROTHY SAYERS"

DAY 1

BEYOND THE EDGE

When we've settled into prosperity and comfort for a
little while we get complacent.—CHIP INGRAM

OKAY, LET'S BE HONEST.

I like adventures, but they've got to be "safe" adventures like
Disneyland or Hawaii or Mexico. Real adventures into risky or
unknown places make me nervous. I know it sounds shallow, but
real adventures make me worry.

What will I eat?

Where will I sleep?

Will it be clean there?

Will I stay healthy?

What if there's an emergency?

How long will I be stuck on the airplane getting to my destination?

The bottom line is this: A real adventure with a real risk lies just
beyond my comfort zone. I hate to admit it, but I like my easy,
comfortable life, where I have little to worry about, where things
are secure, safe, and predictable.

My friend Martin says I should go to India with him to work in an orphanage. My heart goes out to these poor, neglected children who don't have the advantages of children in this country. But I'm already helping to support three orphan children in Guatemala. Another friend, Julius, tells me that God wants me to go to Uganda for ten days. I've heard about amazing and exciting things that are happening in this part of Africa, but I've already sent two checks to that organization. What more do they want? Besides, God hasn't told me to go to either of these places. After all, they are so far away and foreign. And am I sure that these places are safe? There are just too many risks and uncertainties.

Yet deep in my soul something is stirring—something that calls me to an adventure in spite of my anxiety. It paints pictures in my brain of the extraordinary. It tugs and pulls me out of my comfort zone. I desperately want to embrace this adventure, but at the same time, I fight and resist it.

I'm simultaneously excited and terrified.

Yet I don't want an ordinary faith! Ordinary faith isn't worth it. It's average, boring, tolerable, so-so. I don't want an ordinary marriage or an ordinary job or an ordinary life. Why in the world would I accept an ordinary faith? *Ordinary* and *faith* should be mortal enemies, fighting to stay as far as possible from each other. In reality, an ordinary faith may be no faith at all. It is nothing like the faith depicted in the Bible or in the early church.

True faith is something completely incredible and extraordinary. So what has happened to our faith? What has happened to *my* faith? Its heart and soul are lost and its lifeblood drained. But I've stuffed its body with straw and propped it in the corner, pretending with all earnestness and determination that it's still alive.

Faith has become far too convenient and comfortable. I sip it in the morning with my coffee and lounge with it in the evening as I nod off to sleep. I have taken something dynamically supernatural and turned it into something dull and natural. What should be the life-giving core of my existence has become nothing more than an optional add-on. I use it only when I need it or when I feel desperate. Otherwise it's stored away on a closet shelf, collecting dust. I have reconfigured my faith equation into something between obligation, social club, hobby, and life insurance policy.

In this technology-driven, materialistic culture, I'm afraid I have left God out of my faith. Or maybe I have just made him ordinary—stripping him of his mystery and majesty, his awesomeness and absolute power. I have become distracted and oftentimes even hypnotized by the noise and energy and glitter of this world. I act as if this is all there is, becoming attached to and passionate about what I do and what I own.

How could I have forgotten that God is the source of all I need, and that faith is the most amazing, fulfilling adventure I could ever embark upon? A. W. Tozer reminds us in *The Pursuit of God*, "If we truly want to follow God we must seek to be otherworldly."

As I ponder Tozer's quote, I wonder what it really means to be "otherworldly." I live and breathe and work in this world. It's my home. It's where my life happens. This world delights and disgusts me. It's where I raise a family, watch TV, make a living, pull weeds, visit my friends, go to church. This world is everything I know.

But John warned, "Do not love this world nor the things it offers you, for . . . this world is fading away" (1 John 2:15, 17). It's fading away; time is fading away; I'm fading away. Sometimes this thought scares me. When I was a teenager, this kept me awake in the dark of the night, when everything was quiet and I felt most alone. This fear can still haunt me when I think of what I might be losing.

But what if I'm not losing anything that's really worthwhile? What if being otherworldly means gaining all that is ultimately worthwhile? Maybe to be otherworldly means to think beyond all we see and understand and experience. Maybe it means that we'd better not get too comfortable here or start to think this world can offer more than it really can. Maybe it means being willing to take risks and go beyond the limits of this world and all we are familiar with. Maybe that's when life really begins.

People thought he was crazy.

But Bill did it anyway.

In June of 2002 Bill Elliott, a forty-one-year-old writer and therapist, traveled 6,497 miles away from home deep into the Judean desert of Israel. Bill wanted to escape the comforts and distractions of the safe life. He wanted to be otherworldly. He wanted to journey beyond an ordinary faith and fall into the face of God.

Moses went up to the mountain for forty days and nights to hear God's voice. Elijah traveled forty days and nights through the southern wilderness near Mount Sinai to find God. Jesus was led by God into the Judean wilderness for forty days and nights to be tempted by Satan.

Therefore Bill decided to spend forty days and nights alone on an isolated plateau overlooking the Dead Sea. This was Bill's "lonesome, individual adventure" toward an extraordinary faith. Bill yearned to deepen his spiritual awareness. So he set up his ten-year-old green and white six-foot-by-six-foot dome tent and filled it with four hundred pounds of gear and water. Then Bill waited for God.

This place was not comfortable, but God was worth it. Bill made himself uncomfortable so that his mind and spirit could be sharper. He was surrounded by challenges: intense heat of 125 degrees, deep loneliness, eerie silence, prolonged boredom, general exhaustion. And then there were the animals—scorpions, snakes, mosquitoes, yellow jackets, and flies by the hundreds.

In *Falling into the Face of God*, Bill wrote that he went to the desert to confront God, to meet his "God-edge" and go beyond it.

"We all have an edge. A place we won't go near or look beyond. Or don't want to look into. Or admit is there," he wrote. Most of us stay away from our edges. I know I do. I like to rest safely and comfortably in the middle, where there is little danger or risk—or life. But faith blossoms on the edge. For the edge reminds me that I'm not in control—God is.

To journey near the edge is itself an adventure. Most of us are like J. R. R. Tolkien's description of hobbits: "They never had any adventures or did anything unexpected." Yet with the proper challenge, Bilbo Baggins moved toward the edge and beyond. As a result, he discovered how small and limited and ordinary his world had been.

I think most of us have fallen asleep and grown complacent far from our edge. But being comfortable is dangerous! For comfort leads to mediocrity, and mediocrity leads to nothing.

So often I go through the ordinary motions of life, and even the ordinary motions of faith, but it has all become common and routine and safe. I can do it with my eyes closed and my thoughts somewhere else. Faith has lost its practical, everyday significance, and thus its energy, ecstasy, and ability to excite. I'm afraid I've become dull and boring because I don't understand what I have. Far from my edge, I have no opportunity to fall into the face of God.

As Annie Dillard, the Pulitzer prize–winning author, wrote, "Does anyone have the foggiest idea what sort of power we so blithely invoke?" I'm sitting in the shadow of the sacred and strolling through the splendor of the supernatural without the slightest sense of what surrounds me.

Deep in my heart I know that something is missing and that this isn't how it was meant to be. I know that God is the only one who can satisfy my soul. Yet more often than not, I'm like a sleepwalker who, being out of touch with reality, stumbles past my faith into a dark night that has nothing meaningful to offer. I sell my soul to my stuff and make this world my one and only home.

Now don't get me wrong. I like my house, with its easy chair, television, and cozy fireplace. These things aren't bad; they just don't get me where I want to go. They give me roots when I need wings. They lull me into a false reality of safety and complacency, but this is the death of faith. And ultimately the death of me.

Faith is not a place; it is a journey—a risky journey that takes us beyond all we can see and hear and feel into a supernatural relationship with the maker and caretaker of the universe. God has planted eternity in our hearts, and we will never be satisfied with the natural or the ordinary. We were made for so much more. Jesus said, "My purpose is to give them a rich and satisfying life" (John 10:10). And this life comes through faith—the most extraordinary faith we can ever imagine.

God is always leading us somewhere. Every good journey involves a willingness to follow him into that somewhere. A willingness to take the risk, to throw off the bowline and sail from our protected harbors toward some unknown edge far away in the fog, beyond what is comfortable, convenient, or even conventional.

Each new day we stand precariously on the edge of the extraordinary. Possibilities stretch out before us that are utterly amazing, but we're usually too afraid to look. Instead, we stand with our eyes squeezed shut, clinging with all our might to the solid ground upon which we're most comfortable.

This fear is paralyzing. It keeps us from living. Yet Søren Kierkegaard reminds us that "without risk there is no faith." An extraordinary faith loves risk, for in risk we learn to trust our God more deeply.

But trusting God as we avoid the edges is no trust at all. It is but an illusion built on sweet words and shallow serenity. Trust is only authentic when it is tested and tried. We're standing on the edge with our toes hanging over. If we truly want to experience this thing called faith, we have no choice but to jump.

As he reflects on his time in the desert, Bill Elliott wrote, "I am just a human being who prays for the guidance and courage to jump in, to go toward God." Bill went to the desert to face the fears that kept him from the edge.

But in the desert he learned to jump.

DAY 2

BEYOND FEAR

Only those who risk going too far can possibly find out how far one can go.—T. S. ELIOT

HEIGHTS MAKE ME NERVOUS.

I'm not a fearful person. I can handle most situations. I grit my teeth and gut my way through them. Except when it comes to heights—heights terrify me. I get over twelve feet high on a ladder and my legs shake so much that the ladder is ready to collapse. My stomach tightens and I start to sweat. My mind races through every worst-case scenario and I freeze. I desperately want to be down with my feet on solid ground as quickly as possible.

I trust God, but I really don't like uncomfortable situations. A few months ago, however, some friends asked me to participate in an activity that would stretch my comfort zone. I immediately said yes, figuring this would be a fantastic opportunity to face my fears. But the closer I got to the date of the event, the more uncomfortable I became.

Why did I agree to such a stupid idea? I've got a very busy schedule, and I don't really have the time to deal with this right now. In theory I believe that stretching oneself is a great idea. It's just the practical, personal application that I struggle with.

I sat on the ground in Mount Hood National Forest and looked high into the air at a log that stretched thirty feet between two trees. The guide said, "I want each of you to climb this tree and walk across that log up there." I stared at the log and then stared at the guide thinking, *This guy is crazy. There is no way I'm doing this.* Out on that log I'd have nothing to hold on to, nothing to help keep my balance. On top of that, it was at least a twenty-two-foot drop to the ground. I was sure I couldn't do it, and I begged God to either get me out of it or calm my fears.

He didn't get me out of it. As I slowly climbed the tree, I could feel my heart pounding.

God, help me.

I kept moving upward until I reached the horizontal log.

God, give me strength.

I cautiously shifted my weight onto the log, still holding tightly to the tree.

God, give me courage.

I stood on the log, but I refused to look down. I knew I had to let go of the tree, but I couldn't. I clung to its trunk. It felt solid and safe. If I let go, I might fall.

God, give me faith.

I looked down and saw my buddy, who was holding on to a cable attached to my harness. If I fell, he would catch me.

Okay, God, I'm going to do this.

I loosened my grip, turned away from the security of the tree, and stepped out onto the log. With my eyes focused on the other tree thirty feet away and my arms stretched out for balance, I walked across the log. God calmed my fears and held my hand and helped me do something I thought was impossible. It may sound like a little thing, but for me it was pretty big.

This world is filled with danger and risk. There is always something scary just around the corner, waiting to jump out and grab us. Yet this exercise taught me that I don't need to run or hide. I can actually lean into my fears. Look them in the eyes and smile. What are you afraid of?

+ failure?
+ discomfort?
+ rejection?
+ disappointment?
+ the unknown?

Fear is a part of life. When we run from our fears, we run from life. When we embrace them, we embrace life. This provides us with a new way of looking at the world and all it contains. To risk nothing is to refuse to learn and grow and to miss out on the best of love and life. To live is to risk. Any journey that leads to a place of value will have its risks. I want to leap into the adventure with a courage that outshines my fears.

The spiritual life is a journey beyond what is familiar and safe into the mysterious and sometimes scary world of the Spirit. It requires a willingness to say good-bye to the ordinary and sail beyond life as we know it toward a deeper, grander reality. This is the strange land of faith, where unspeakable beauty and unpredictable danger mingle in the miraculous.

I really want to experience authentic faith, but doing so means I must let go of my preconceived notions and expectations. I must launch into the deep, with my back to the shore, and trust that

God will use this journey to bring me closer to him. Don't get me wrong. What's on the shore is sometimes very good. But everything there—all I have learned and seen and believed—is only the beginning of the journey. This amazing, exciting, terrifying quest promises to stretch me to the very edge of who I am and what I know. My past has prepared me for this point in time. Now I must move beyond fear and rest in his promises to never let me down.

Are you ready to join me? Fear will offer you hundreds of logical and practical reasons *not* to take this journey. Why leave the safety and security of what you know for who-knows-what?

But what if safety and security are antithetical to extraordinary faith?

What if the supernatural universe is more real than all we can see and feel and understand?

What if Thomas à Kempis, a fourteenth-century German monk, was right when he said that we are never safe in this life?

What if the only way to be safe is to look beyond this life and trust the incomprehensible, the invisible, and the impossible?

If there were charts or formulas for this priceless, perilous journey, there would be no need for faith.

Habakkuk lived in Judah some six hundred years before Christ during a difficult time in the country's history. He was filled with questions and often cried out for answers. He wanted God to fix everything and return life to peace and affluence. But God had something else in mind. He took away Habakkuk's comfort and security, leading him to the very edge and forcing him to look beyond. Habakkuk wrote, "I trembled inside . . . my lips quivered with fear. My legs gave way beneath me, and I shook in terror" (Habakkuk 3:16).

In spite of his fears, Habakkuk stepped up to the challenge. He did not flee or raise his fist in anger. Instead, he saw the obstacles before him as an opportunity to deepen his faith and draw closer to God. In fact, his final thoughts in the short book that bears his name, read: "The Sovereign LORD is my strength! He makes me as surefooted as a deer, able to tread upon the heights" (Habakkuk 3:19).

Thinking back on my walk twenty feet above the ground, I have to agree with Habakkuk. For even when I'm fearful, God can lead me upon the heights. He can lead me to the very edge and over it. He is my strength and comfort. No matter what.

DAY 3

BEYOND COMPREHENSION

The world dwarfs us all, but God dwarfs the world.

—J. I. PACKER

"I DON'T KNOW," I WHISPERED UNDER MY BREATH.

I closed my eyes and felt the frustration building. I looked at the problem again and tried to concentrate, but the equation with all its numbers and letters just didn't make any sense to me. It was like some mystical language my brain simply could not absorb. I was fourteen years old, and this advanced algebra class was driving me crazy. The more I concentrated and tried to figure out the problems, the more confused I became. I studied every day and even got extra help from the teacher twice a week, but I continued to struggle with the concepts, and my head continued to hurt.

At that point it was confirmed that I would never be a mathematical genius. I had hit the limit of my understanding. Nearly forty years later, math still does not come easily to me, and sometimes it doesn't come at all. We all have areas of life we don't understand. Even math experts can't figure out *every* formula or theorem. Not knowing or understanding is just a part of the human condition. But our culture prizes knowledge to such a degree that although we live in a world of obscurity and ambiguity, we grow nervous when we move beyond the knowable. We feel uncomfortable with the things we can't explain. If things are too far beyond our comfort zones, we resist them and ignore them and sometimes even lash out against them.

But what if those very things are blessings sent to teach us about our marvelous limitations?

What if they are lessons designed to undermine our pride and arrogance?

What if they are gifts from God to make us humble and draw us closer to him?

I am the first to admit that some things are simply incomprehensible—in part because there is so much I don't comprehend, from the depths of the ocean to the heights of outer space. In fact, there are times I don't even seem to know myself. As a psychologist, I realize that a healthy person learns to approach the unknown and make peace with the incomprehensible. To assume that I must avoid things I don't understand is both shortsighted and ridiculous. I don't understand how a television works, but that doesn't stop me from watching it. I don't know how certain foods are made, but that doesn't keep me from eating them. I don't comprehend the ways of God, but that doesn't cause me to distance myself from him.

Faith is a bold step into the unknown. It is an acknowledgment that our thoughts are too human, too small, too limited to comprehend the ways of God. God is so vast that our thoughts get lost in his immensity. At best we might grasp but a splinter of his splendor or a glimpse of his character. So minuscule is the slice of reality we can see that it can only be compared to a hazy shadow of a distant reflection of his magnificent glory.

God is beyond comprehension and imagination. To reduce him to the level of human understanding is to take away much of what makes him God. For how can a finite mind ever comprehend an infinite God? King David sang out, "Great is the LORD! . . . No one can measure his greatness" (Psalm 145:3). And the prophet Isaiah asked rhetorically, "Who has understood the mind of the LORD?" (Isaiah 40:13, NIV).

One of Job's tormentors rightly said, "The Almighty is beyond our reach" (Job 37:23, NIV). Even so, we still need to strive to know all we can know, regardless of how limited that knowledge may be. For even the smallest drop of water can be enormously refreshing to a thirsty soul.

I do not need to fully understand God to walk with him. I simply need to relax and let him amaze me with his greatness. Donald Miller wrote in *Blue Like Jazz*, "It comforts me to think that if we are created beings, the thing that created us would have to be greater than us, so much greater, in fact, that we would not be able to understand it."

I don't want an ordinary God any more than I want an ordinary faith. Ordinary might make me feel good, but it will never inspire and astound me. Only an extraordinary God can move me beyond complacency in such a way that I cannot help but be changed.

When I truly consider and contemplate the creator of eternity and infinity, I'm shaken to my very core. If he is comprehensible, I need not change; but if he is incomprehensible, I would be foolish *not* to change. In the end C. S. Lewis was right: "The best is perhaps what we understand least." And what I understand least is frequently what moves me most.

DAY 4

BEYOND THE VISIBLE

Faith tells us of things we have never seen, and cannot come to know by our natural senses.

—SAINT JOHN OF THE CROSS

COMPLETE AND UTTER DARKNESS IS REALLY SCARY.

When I was a child my family took a guided tour through some caves in Idaho. In one of the deepest caverns, the guide turned off his light to show us what real darkness was like. It was pitch-black. I couldn't even see my hand as I waved it in front of my face. After a few moments I could feel the fear rising.

"Mom? Dad? Is anybody here?" Immediately they both responded, and I knew I wasn't alone. Even though I couldn't see them, I knew everything was okay.

Much of life is like that: beyond the visible. And a certain amount of life is beyond the security of our other senses as well.

Moses had the ability to stretch beyond his senses to see a deeper, more powerful, more accurate reality. The writer of Hebrews said, "It was by faith that Moses left the land of Egypt. . . . He kept right on going because he kept his eyes on the one who is invisible" (Hebrews 11:27).

Looking beyond the visible doesn't seem natural. We use sight and sound and touch to survive in this world, but I wonder if it's possible to trust our senses too much. What if what we perceive through our senses is only the thinnest layer of life?

Common wisdom says that if I can't see it, hear it, feel it, smell it, or taste it, it can't be real. But my five senses are merely God-given gifts that help me navigate the challenging and charming aspects of this natural world. In reality, the senses have significant limits.

At our core, we are spiritual beings living in a supernatural universe. My senses can only take me so far. As the apostle Paul wrote, "We live by faith, not by sight" (2 Corinthians 5:7, NIV). At least we *should* live by faith, not by sight. Faith takes us beyond the limitations of our senses and shows us possibilities that stretch our imaginations in unthinkable directions—supernatural directions.

True reality is not contingent upon physical experiences. These are but the skin of an apple or the peel of an orange. The outside may be beautiful or frustrating, but I can only experience its reality when I get past the external layer into the fruit. It's faith that takes the bite. Only then do I find that the spiritual has been surrounding me and embracing me all the time. While I played silly games and chased beloved dreams, true reality has been patiently and consistently calling me to a deeper, fuller life, beyond all I can see.

In his profound wisdom, God frequently provides sensory hints of another world. He pulls back the curtain to give a quick glimpse of the beauty and grandeur of the supernatural. Everything seen originates in what is unseen, for the invisible is the real power behind the visible.

Ralph Waldo Emerson said, "All I have seen teaches me to trust the Creator for all I have not seen." This thought turns my world upside down and challenges everything I've been taught, but it is true. The visible is real, but the invisible is *more real*. Therefore Paul said, "So we fix our eyes not on what is seen, but on what is unseen" (2 Corinthians 4:18, NIV).

To move beyond the visible is to not be controlled or tempted by the superficial, regardless of how powerful and alluring it may feel. It is to remind myself that this life is temporary and to move my focus onto what is more substantial.

We have all been indoctrinated by the idea that seeing is believing, but in reality just the opposite is true: Believing is seeing. And as the writer of Hebrews proclaimed, "Now faith is being . . . certain of what we do not see" (Hebrews 11:1, NIV).

There are so many things I cannot see: wind, warmth, love, angels, demons, God's hand. Yet these things actually have the greatest power. And if I can't seem to capture even the invisible things I *know* about, how can I even begin to catch the rest?

In so many ways, I feel like the blind man in the city of Bethsaida. I am blind but I really want to see. Jesus understands this predicament. He took the blind man by the hand and led him out of the city, away from the security and distractions of the world as he knew it. God moved this man from the middle out to the very edge. Then Jesus touched his eyes and asked, "Can you see anything now?"

What a great question! *Can I see anything now?* Can I see beyond my natural vision? Can I see with a supernatural vision that takes me beyond this world, introducing an infinite array of unexpected images with new colors, new textures, and new dimensions?

I want Jesus to touch my eyes, my mind, my heart. I want fresh eyes to see with a vividness that transports me far beyond the foggy lands of the visible.

The blind man looked around and said to Jesus, "Yes, I see . . . but I can't see . . . very clearly." Most of the time I can't see very clearly either. But every once in a while I catch a momentary flash of color that tells me there is much, much more to see, to hear, to touch.

Someday in this world or the next, I believe we will all truly see. Jesus reached out and touched the blind man's eyes a second time. The Gospel of Mark reports that then "he could see everything clearly" (Mark 8:25).

Oh, if Jesus would just touch me more. His first touch opened my eyes, but only in a blurry squint—with everything dim and distorted and undefined. My heart yearns for that second touch, for that is when I will truly see beyond the visible. That is when I will see things as they truly are, apart from this heavy fog I walk in daily. I want to peer past this physical empire, beyond its trite tangibility and vacant visions. For then I will finally know that I have never really seen anything at all.

DAY 5

BEYOND THE POSSIBLE

May thy grace, O Lord, make that possible to me which seems impossible to me by nature.—AMY CARMICHAEL

IT'S IMPOSSIBLE.

I believe this is one of the most foolish phrases a person can ever utter. During my fifty-plus years of walking this planet, I have experienced much that seemed beyond the possible. As a logical and pragmatic person, I have often thought of something as impossible and boldly stated it as such, only to have to eat my words as I watched a guaranteed impossibility blossom into a full-fledged reality right before my eyes. (I often wonder how many other things have become reality beyond my awareness and vision as well.)

Yes, I've lived too long to keep myself trapped in the dull land of the possible. You can call them random coincidences, lucky breaks, or just freak accidents. But I call them miracles—impossibilities that, against all odds, become possibilities. We live in a world full of miracles.

God is not bound by the natural, the rational, or the imaginable. He often chooses to work within these parameters, but he might just as easily make his mark within the realm of the supernatural, the irrational, or the unimaginable. For him all things are possible, even that which is impossible. Jesus tells us, "With man this is impossible, but with God all things are possible" (Matthew 19:26, NIV). To the immense, infinite, and eternal God, there are no impossibilities—nothing that is beyond his capability, understanding, or imagination.

Risky faith takes me into the spiritual realm, where there are no limits. Reason and logic can only take me so far. Reason is important, but if I rest solely on reason, I become trapped in the natural world of black and white. Faith beyond reason boldly offers a vibrant world of breathtaking color. Consider the following:

+ Enoch disappeared into the heavens.
+ Abraham had a son when he was one hundred years old.
+ Moses parted the Red Sea, walking across on dry land.
+ Daniel stood unsinged in a fiery furnace.
+ Elijah brought a boy back from death.
+ Jesus fed five thousand people with five loaves and two fish.

Maybe F. B. Meyer was right when he wrote, "We never test the resources of God until we attempt the impossible."

Ordinary faith, nurtured by reason and practicality, hesitates at the impossible. The dream is too big, the mountain is too high, the need is too great, the person is too closed. It doesn't make sense, things don't work that way, the risk is too great. I often tremble at the obstacles rather than celebrate the opportunities. I forget that I am not alone and that God can't wait to show me his hand.

Lewis Carroll, who wrote the children's classic *Through the Looking-Glass and What Alice Found There*, discovered the joy of impossibilities.

"I can't believe *that*!" said Alice.

"Can't you?" the Queen said in a pitying tone. "Try again: draw a long breath, and shut your eyes."

Alice laughed. "There's no use in trying," she said: "one *can't* believe impossible things."

"I daresay you haven't had much practice," said the Queen. "When I was your age, I always did it for half-an-hour a day. Why, sometimes I've believed as many as six impossible things before breakfast."

What if we all decided to believe six impossible things before breakfast? What if we all did just one impossible thing each day? How would it change our lives?

An extraordinary faith in an extraordinary God refuses to back down.

Even when we risk extraordinary faith, we may not ever feel comfortable with the impossible; we simply trust the One who does the impossible. Extraordinary faith stretches into the uncomfortable in order to embrace the supernatural. Andrew Murray, a nineteenth-century Scottish pastor, wrote that our lives are "every day to be a proof that God works impossibilities."

What if Christians across the world really took this seriously?

What if we challenged every impossibility?

What if we practiced extraordinary faith?

How many dreams would come true?

How many mountains would be moved?

How many needs would be met?

How many lives would be changed?

I want to live a full life. I want to have the courage to walk to the edge. I want to do the impossible. Yet the line from the movie

Braveheart haunts me: "Every man dies; not every man really lives." To really live is to grow and stretch beyond the artificial boundaries of logic and experience. These boundaries work well within a natural universe, but when I reach into the realm of the supernatural, these preconceived boundaries actually reinforce my blindness. To live is to move beyond myself, my fear, my limits. Only then will I really see what God can do.

As each year passes I continue to be shocked and amazed at what God does. He often provides new and unexpected opportunities that pull me from my comfort zone and into something extraordinary. God never fails. He loves to take me further than I ever thought possible. Much of what I do now I would have thought impossible ten years ago. God is constantly, patiently waiting for me to step further into a world of impossibilities. That is where the excitement really begins, for that is where life really begins.

DAY 6

SETTING SAIL

IT SEEMS STUPID TO FIGHT GOD.

Yet I do it more often than I care to admit. God nudges me to pray more, give more, help more, *be* more. These are all things I strongly believe in, but I find reasons not to do them—good, respectable, solid reasons. I want to walk the edges and borders that put me face-to-face with God, but my feet tend to keep to the well-trod paths of everyday life. I rarely move into uncharted territory unless it is well thought out, so as to minimize the risks. Yet to move beyond the middle, away from the broad road, starts with willingness—a willingness to step out of the status quo, to risk, to stretch, to be uncomfortable.

Daily I struggle to let go of all that is safe, comfortable, and reasonable. At times this seems too risky and challenging. Yet it is only at the edge that I can drink from the water of life and fall into the hands of God.

In Spain, after Columbus discovered the New World, coins were created bearing the Latin slogan *Plus Ultra*, which means "more beyond." This is the horizon-expanding message to all who are tired of the ordinary and yearn for something more. There is more—much more. All we need to do is sail forward with the excitement and anticipation that there is truly "more beyond."

Stepping beyond the ordinary frequently begins with a simple willingness—a willingness to embrace that there is "more beyond." Sometimes God takes us far away and sometimes he brings far away to us. Reaching out to those possibilities right in front of you might feel like a baby step, but it's a beginning. And that's where we need to start.

VERSE TO REMEMBER

The gateway to life is very narrow and the road is difficult, and only a few ever find it.—MATTHEW 7:14

QUESTIONS TO PONDER

+ When you see the narrow gate, how does it make you feel? Does this faith seem too hard, too challenging to risk?

+ What are the fears that keep you from a risking faith? How have these been blocking you and what might you do to "move beyond" your current faith?

+ What would it take to move you beyond the comprehensible, the visible, and the possible?

QUOTE TO INSPIRE

"Disturb us, O Lord, when . . . we arrived safely because we sailed too close to the shore. . . . Disturb us, Lord, to dare move boldly, to venture on wider seas . . . where losing sight of land, we shall find the stars."—SIR FRANCIS DRAKE

02 | GET REAL

"We are all afraid of reality; we pretend to want to know ourselves, and we are afraid of knowing ourselves."

—PAUL TOURNIER

DAY 7

RUTHLESS HONESTY

> When I get honest . . . I believe and I doubt, I hope and
> get discouraged, I love and I hate, I feel bad about feeling
> good, I feel guilty about not feeling guilty. I am trusting
> and suspicious. I am honest and I still play games.
>
> —BRENNAN MANNING

IT WAS SO BIG, I COULDN'T BELIEVE IT!

When I was ten years old I saw the Pacific Ocean for the first time. We had been driving through the mountains of northern Oregon when we turned a corner and . . . there it was. The largest body of water I had ever seen. An hour later I stood with my feet buried in the sand at Cannon Beach and just stared at the western horizon. Water stretched out in front of me as far as I could see.

"Where does it end?" I asked.

"As far as China," my father answered. He might as well have said Venus or Mars, for they all seemed a million miles away. As I stood looking into the distance at this big ocean, I felt smaller than I had ever felt.

As I've grown older and more calloused, however, I think I've lost that feeling. I've become blind to the obvious realities surrounding me, and somehow in my foolishness, the ocean seems smaller than it really is and I seem grander. What a strange optical illusion! Oh, if only I could recapture the honesty and innocence I had as a child.

Once in a while, I feel it again. When I look up at the stars on a crystal clear night, I am keenly aware that God is amazingly great and I am surprisingly small. Carlo Carreto wrote, "There are moments when God makes us feel the extreme limits of our powerlessness; then, and only then, do we understand our nothingness right down to the depths." These Grand Canyon moments help me to keep who I am in perspective.

Let's face it. We are small people who live a small stretch of time on a small planet that circles a small sun in an immense universe.

Early astronomers believed the universe revolved around the earth. But in the sixteenth century when Nicolaus Copernicus suggested that the earth is not the center of the universe, he knew people would be outraged. How could anyone think such a ludicrous thing and defy popular opinion? Yet Copernicus was right. The universe does not revolve around us—our thoughts, our plans, our desires. Rick Warren opened his best-selling classic, *The Purpose-Driven Life*, with the words, "It's not about you."

Ruthless honesty forces me to face the truth of who I really am, stripped of all facades, pretense, and pride. This may be uncomfortable or frightening, but I know that if I cannot accept my own brokenness I cannot grow. Like all of humanity, I am flawed at every level: physical, mental, emotional, social, and spiritual.

Yet Mark Buchanan, a Canadian pastor and author, reminds us, "Brokenness—a broken heart, a broken spirit—molds our character closer to the character of God than anything else." I have found this to be so true in my life. When all is going well, I tend to lean on myself. But when things get broken, I become desperate to lean on God—his help or wisdom or protection.

This world is full of brokenness—broken hearts, broken bodies, broken relationships, broken promises, broken rules, and broken trust. Sooner or later, everything gets broken. At some level, I think we all recognize this, but even so, we still have a strong tendency to deny, minimize, and cover up our brokenness.

Therefore, the first step in risking a deeper faith involves being totally honest about the fact that I am broken before a flawless God. Paul tells us to "be honest in your evaluation of yourselves" (Romans 12:3). I may be noble, creative, and rational, but ruthless honesty tells me that I am also broken:

I am finite. I have limitations and weaknesses at every level.
I am mortal. My body will fail me and I will die.
I am imperfect. I have flaws that show up every day.
I am incomplete. I cannot do all that I want on my own.
I am sinful. I do and think unhealthy, hurtful things.
I am fragile. I get hurt, sick, or out of balance.
I am fearful. I grow anxious about all sorts of things, big and little.

Sometimes I think I do pretty well. I'm patient and wise and kind. I say the right thing at the right time, I keep my mouth shut and listen when I need to, and I go out of my way to help someone. But then there are all those times that I don't do any of those things. And if I'm really honest, I have to admit that most of the time, I'm not nearly as good as I pretend to be.

Jimmy was a skateboarder.

We lived in the same neighborhood, and I went to school with his big brother. When I was fifteen he was just a kid, maybe five years younger than I was. Jimmy was an obnoxious kid, constantly bragging about how he was the best skateboarder in North America. We usually just told him to shut up and go home. But one hot summer afternoon, as a bunch of the neighborhood guys were hanging out and waiting for the ice cream truck to come by, Jimmy challenged me to a skateboarding contest. All my friends were watching and I didn't want to lose face, so I agreed.

I don't know what I was thinking. I had never stepped foot on a board in my life, and I had never seen Jimmy in public without his board. But somehow I decided I was going to teach this kid a lesson. I wanted to take him down a notch and show him I could do anything he could do.

We followed Jimmy to his driveway, which was the longest and steepest in the neighborhood, trading trash talk all the way there. Jimmy and I were psyched up and ready for the battle. Jimmy went first and he performed flawlessly. The neighborhood kids cheered. "Traitors," I muttered under my breath. Then I gritted my teeth, climbed on the board someone had loaned me, and took off. I stayed on the board nearly halfway down the driveway (which was a miracle), but as I did, I kept moving faster and faster. I was feeling pretty good when suddenly I hit a small rock. The board stopped and I went sailing forward, face-first onto the concrete sidewalk at the end of the driveway.

My lower lip was swollen and bleeding. My hands were scraped up and stung like crazy. I had a gash on my forehead. My body ached, but the most painful thing was having to swallow my pride and concede that little, obnoxious Jimmy had beaten me.

It's really hard for me to admit that I'm not very good at something. Accepting defeat can be humiliating. I think we all have egos that sometimes get the best of us. I know I do. I'd like to think that I can do certain things better, faster, or more efficiently than others. I want to be important. I want to be above average, at least in something.

Sometimes I really want things to go my way, and I figure that anybody who disagrees with me must be wrong. But this inflated perspective doesn't get me anywhere. Medieval theologian Nicholas of Cusa wrote, "The better a man knows his own ignorance, the greater his learning will be."

Honesty pushes me beyond my ego so I can look in a mirror and capture my reflection as it truly is. I don't always like what I see, and there are times when I'm afraid to look too closely. Sometimes I even start to avoid mirrors altogether. I have a dark side. I have sins and secrets and regrets. I have that embarrassing moment I hope nobody ever discovers. And deep in my heart, I'm afraid that if my real self is exposed, something terrible will happen.

When we avoid the mirror of honesty, we are like Adam and Eve, who made clothes to cover their nakedness and then hid in the trees. Yet we need not hide; God knows our every weakness and fault. He is looking for us, calling our names, and asking, "Where are you?" He is seeking us, not to punish us, but to embrace us.

God wants to make me healthy, and that requires that I admit the obvious. God has already seen it and accepted it. He merely asks me to be ruthlessly honest and let him work through me. He promises to reshape all my imperfections and weaknesses: "My power works best in weakness" (2 Corinthians 12:9). Who can argue with that?

U2 lead singer Bono once said, "That the Scriptures are brim full of hustlers, murderers, cowards, adulterers and mercenaries used to shock me. Now it is a source of great comfort." The Bible certainly does not inflate or whitewash its heroes:

+ Noah drank too much.
+ Abraham lied.
+ Sarah was a whiner.
+ Jacob cheated his brother.
+ Moses was a murderer.
+ Samson was a sex addict.
+ Eli failed as a father.
+ David was unfaithful.
+ Elijah wanted to die.
+ Jonah was a selfish coward.

Yet these were all people God sought after. They weren't perfect, but God was able to use them because they simply said yes to an extraordinary adventure with him. We aren't perfect, but God wants to do something amazing with us.

Lately I've made more of an effort to be honest about my weaknesses. And with this increased honesty I've found that there is incredible freedom in admitting my failures. When I'm honest, I'm free to admit that I need help, that I struggle sometimes, and that I will always be below average in certain areas.

Ruthless honesty forces me to lean on God and others. It whispers that I am not the center of the universe. Besides, pretending to have it all together is just too much work.

If little Jimmy challenged me to a skateboarding contest today, I would smile and say, "You're the best." At least if I were smart, I would.

DAY 8

SELFLESS HUMILITY

> If you should ask me what are the ways of God, I would tell you that the first is humility, the second is humility, and the third is still humility. —SAINT AUGUSTINE

WHAT ARE YOU MOST PROUD OF?

Maybe it's your looks or your health or your abilities. Maybe it's some special talent or status. Maybe it's your stuff. I used to be proud of my bright, shiny Nissan Xterra, but now that I've had it for six years it's not so bright and shiny anymore. Even though I've tried to take great care of it, it has little nicks on it, the emergency brake light won't turn off, and the engine is making a strange noise. Stuff breaks.

Some days when I'm writing, the words flow smoothly, the concepts are clear, and I'm proud of what I've done. But not always. I keep showing my writings to a friend of mine. I guess I want his approval or affirmation, or maybe just his respect. I want him to say, "Wow, this is really something!" But he usually just tears apart my logic and my sentences. I know he's not trying to be critical. He's actually very nice and polite about it, but it's clear that he's not impressed. I try not to take this too personally, but sadly enough, it hurts my pride. I know it shouldn't, but it does.

I want to be a great writer, but the reality is that's not how God made me. I know I'm not a bad writer—I can be encouraging and helpful and periodically even thought provoking—but God, in his infinite wisdom, knows that if I were a great writer it would probably go to my head. My pride would smother my humility. So he allows me to be a simple writer who shares truth in relatively simple ways. Maybe when he believes I can handle my pride, God will allow me to write something really great. But it must be his timing, not mine.

Pride brings out the worst in me. It hardens my heart, making me insensitive and critical and cold. As I push myself up, I frequently, without intention, push others down and God out. I am not purposefully proud; it just comes naturally.

Sooner or later, I think pride gets us all. Pride is at the core of all sin and selfishness; it puts us at the center of the universe and then convinces us that we actually deserve this position. But pride is the enemy of humility, and humility is the enemy of pride. James wrote that "God opposes the proud but favors the humble" (James 4:6). James was saying that while God resists and stands against those who are proud, he supports and stands beside those who are humble. I know which side I want to be on; I certainly don't want God to stand against me.

An ordinary faith has self at its core. God is present, but he is there primarily to help me meet *my* potential, overcome *my* difficulties, and find *my* happiness. Our culture says I must take good care of myself. I must be self-aware and develop a positive self-esteem with a sense of self-confidence. These ideas are not unhealthy in themselves, but if we're not careful, they can quickly morph into pride: self-absorption, self-indulgence, and self-importance. Soon everything is about self.

Humility, on the other hand, is not easy and does not come naturally. In this dog-eat-dog, grab-all-you-can world, humility runs counter to culture; it is a lost art. Yet humility is central to an extraordinary faith. Once I finally become ruthlessly honest about God and who he is—good and glorious and grand—and about who I am in light of his amazing immensity, humility is the only sane response.

This sort of humility is love and generosity and sacrifice at their greatest. I know this is what God wants, but it just seems too difficult. There has to be an easier way.

There's not.

Solomon wrote, "With humility comes wisdom" (Proverbs 11:2). What if wisdom can only begin when we recognize we are nothing? What if God wants us to be humble because only in humility do we realize that God is everything?

God completes me. He fills my emptiness and gives me meaning. Humility is the opening of my heart to God. It is the only way to start this mysterious, passionate journey. Peter tells us to "humble yourselves under the mighty power of God" (1 Peter 5:6). To successfully move forward, I have no other option.

To be healthy I must be humble. To be realistic I must be humble. To grow I must be humble. Anything I wish to do with any level of authenticity requires humility: speaking, washing dishes, reading the Bible, answering e-mails, helping a friend, resolving a conflict. Humility has at its base a ruthless honesty.

To be truly humble, we need to resist certain things. If we're humble, we do not:

1. advertise our deeds
2. defend our positions

3. cherish our opinions
4. rehash our words
5. cling to our rights
6. dwell on our appearances
7. worry about our reputations
8. compare our strengths
9. fear our weaknesses
10. love our possessions

Humility lets go of itself. It fights pride with all its might, accepting with ruthless honesty its humanity and freeing us from the trivialities and concerns of this world. Mother Teresa was one of the most humble people of our time. She left her home and country to serve the poorest people in India. She gave all she had and learned that "if you are humble nothing will touch you, neither praise nor disgrace, because you know what you are."

In an intriguing paradox, Mother Teresa learned that the only way to find herself and be fulfilled was to give up on herself. Humility is so powerful because it helps us recognize that we are totally dependent on God and that we are absolutely nothing without him. John recognized this when he said, "He must become greater and greater, and I must become less and less" (John 3:30). We must get out of God's way so he can work in our lives. And as we become less, he becomes greater.

In my own life, every single day I desperately need:

+ his peace
+ his wisdom
+ his strength
+ his guidance

+ his comfort
+ his love
+ his patience
+ his forgiveness

There is beauty and simplicity in a humble heart. Julian of Norwich, a fourteenth-century English mystic, wrote, "For the soul is at its best, its most noble and honorable, when it is most lowly, and humble, and gentle."

The humble give themselves up to God to do with as he wishes. They are willing to become his servants—and because of his love for humanity, servants to all. The heart of a servant diminishes itself so it can lift others up. As Peter tells us, we are to "serve each other in humility" (1 Peter 5:5).

To be humble I have to stop thinking I am better and more important than anyone else. I have to recognize that all I have is a gift from God. Everything can be taken away just as easily as it was given. And if this is true, I have to willingly let go of my pride, my ego, my rights, my opinions, and my preferences. Only then can I truly build others up. Only then can I pray with these words recorded by George Verwer:

> That others might be loved more than I,
> that others might be esteemed more than I,
> that . . . others might be chosen and I set aside,
> that others might be preferred to me in everything.

The greatest example of humility this world has ever seen is Jesus. He spent his life serving others—helping, healing, teaching, encouraging, and feeding the various people he came in contact with. Jesus' philosophy was, "Whoever wants to be a leader among you must be your servant, and whoever wants to be first among you must be the slave of everyone else" (Mark 10:43-44). Clothed in humility, Jesus reached out to those the culture ignored: outcasts, widows, orphans, lepers, tax collectors, prostitutes, foreigners, criminals, and the poor. Jesus did not worry about status or position or rights; he cared only about others. He was rejected and ridiculed, but he served anyway.

In the end he died a criminal's death on a cross, the ultimate symbol of humility. I find it difficult to be proud when I think of the simple life of Jesus. I find it even more difficult when I stand at the foot of the Cross and consider all he experienced—the beatings, the spikes that were driven through his hands, the thorny crown, the ridicule he endured, the spear forced into his side, the painful death he willingly suffered.

All of this, when he had done nothing wrong.

Maybe Charles Spurgeon said it best when he wrote, "Abide close to the cross and search the mystery of His wounds." Maybe this is the key to humility.

Maybe it's also the key to a real faith.

DAY 9

DESPERATE CONFESSION

> Sin is . . . an act of supreme ingratitude . . . an act of
> defiance . . . a rebellious act in which we are setting
> ourselves in opposition to the One to whom we owe
> everything.—R. C. SPROUL

I WAS DESPERATE.

Several years after God woke me up in the middle of the night with that rotten airplane trick, I started to panic. *What if I wasn't sincere enough? What if I said it all wrong? What if fear was a poor motivation?* I must have been about ten years old at the time, and every night when I crawled into bed, my mind went wild. I would think about all the things I'd done wrong during the day and the Bible verse my fourth-grade Sunday school teacher had taught us: "If we confess our sins, he is faithful and just to forgive us our sins, and to cleanse us from all unrighteousness" (1 John 1:9, KJV).

I was excited by the thought that I could have all the gruff and grime of life washed away by simply confessing. So, lying on my back in my twin-size bed, I would squeeze my eyes tightly shut and confess every sin and failure I could remember. Then I confessed everything I couldn't remember and then all the things I might have done wrong but didn't know were wrong. And I didn't stop there! I even confessed any of my previous prayers of confession that might not have been done properly. For the next year or so I went through these prayers each night, hoping that if any of my previous confessions didn't work, this particular confession would cover me.

As a kid, I was certainly too anxious about confession. As an adult, I've since come to understand that God's grace is sufficient enough to cover all my sins, in spite of my limited memory and vocabulary. But unfortunately, now that I'm older, I sometimes go to the opposite extreme, not taking confession seriously enough.

And I don't think I'm alone. Many Christians today view confession as trite or irrelevant—an antiquated, unnecessary ritual. We no longer see confession as a crucial part of our spiritual hygiene. We value a clean body over a clean soul, and then wonder why we feel no peace. But confession makes us clean. Just as we need to shower or bathe on a regular basis, we also need to confess on a regular basis if we want to be emotionally, intellectually, and spiritually clean.

Life is a struggle—a struggle to do the right thing, the loving thing, the healthy thing, the generous thing, the meaningful thing, the humble thing. Yet so much of the time I end up doing the easy thing or the comfortable thing or the selfish thing. Then, rather than confessing my failure, I attempt to justify my actions, when they are actually just one more example of my desperation.

I am broken and long to be fixed, unhealthy and long to be healed, guilty and long to be forgiven. I try to hide from these facts through denial and distraction. Or I try to run from them through busyness and activity. But sooner or later, my human condition always breaks through. And when it does, I realize just how desperate I truly am.

But desperation is not necessarily a bad thing. Desperation reminds me that without God I am lost. When I am in danger I don't hesitate to cry out to God, but when all is calm God is no longer crucial. Or so I think.

It's difficult for me to admit a constant dependence on anything, even God. It makes me feel weak and vulnerable. I don't like it. I want to prove to the world that I can do things on my own. Yet without God's nudging and assistance, I am capable of nothing. Oh, sometimes it looks like I'm doing great on my own, but it's only an illusion. Unfortunately, even I sometimes fall for my own illusion. Delusion and deception give me a false sense of independence. I know in my heart that this is not where I want to go, but my cockiness and inflated sense of identity pull me into the following foolish thinking patterns:

+ *I can do it myself, and I don't need anybody's help.*
+ *I like it my way, and I don't care what anybody else says.*
+ *I will do what gets me ahead and feels good.*
+ *I am better, smarter, and more capable than most.*

All these attitudes are empty and ultimately unsatisfying. They are selfish, sinful, and stupid. They take me further and further from God, leaving me more desperate than when I began.

We all sin. Solomon wrote, "Not a single person on earth is always good and never sins" (Ecclesiastes 7:20).

When it comes to sinning, I'm more consistent with this than I am with eating breakfast and lunch (and I'm pretty consistent with both of those things). I have questioned a lot about my faith over the years, but one thing I've never questioned, not even for a moment, is the fact that I sin.

I learned right from wrong early. I also learned that wrong seemed to be a lot more fun. One night when I was eight I tiptoed into the kitchen very softly so I wouldn't wake up my parents. I climbed onto the counter and reached into the cupboard where the chocolate chip cookies were crying out to me. Now I knew the rules well: *No chocolate chip cookies unless you ask* and *No more than three at a time.* Even so, I pulled my pajama top open at the neck and piled handful after handful into the material. Then the conviction hit me. *This is wrong. I shouldn't be taking these cookies.* I bowed my head and asked God to forgive me for what I was doing. Then I ran off to my room to eat my cookies. I knew that this was a sin, but I *really* wanted those cookies.

Things haven't changed much over the past forty years. I still want to break the rules if they keep me from getting what I want. I'm just a lot more subtle and sneaky and sophisticated about it than I used to be. I tell myself things like:

+ *It doesn't really matter.*
+ *Nobody cares.*
+ *It's my body and I can do whatever I want with it.*
+ *It's not like I'm hurting anybody.*
+ *Everybody does it.*
+ *There's nothing really wrong with it.*

In the end I try to convince myself that it's just a little sin.

But what exactly is sin? The Greek word for *sin* means "to miss the mark."

Susanna Wesley, mother of John and Charles Wesley, described sin this way: "Whatever weakens your reasoning, impairs the tenderness of your conscience, obscures your sense of God or takes away your relish for spiritual things . . . that to you becomes sin, however good it is in itself."

James put it in more practical terms: "Remember, it is sin to know what you ought to do and then not do it" (James 4:17).

Sin scars the soul. It keeps us from our potential and separates us from God, others, and ourselves. Eugene Peterson, a poet and a professor, tells us that "sin is diminishing, dehumanizing, and soon dull."

Fortunately for us, it is possible to move beyond the cycle of sin and into a cycle of confession. The more honest I am with myself, the more I realize that I need help. Opening up and confessing my brokenness and sin brings me closer to God, and the closer I get to him the more aware I become of my brokenness and sin. This is the cycle of confession.

Richard Foster, a well-known Quaker writer, wrote, "The discipline of confession brings an end to pretense. . . . Honesty leads to confession, and confession leads to change." The opposite of confession is being closed—shutting myself in and ultimately shutting down. Confession is the only path to freedom and forgiveness.

Since we are all guilty, we all need confession. Yet true confession is painful and frightening. We must look at the darkness of our hearts and listen to the desperate stirrings of our souls. We must swallow our pride and drop our defenses so that we might be humble, vulnerable, and completely real. Then we can follow our desperation into the helplessness that recognizes the fact that absolute confession is the only way out.

Whenever I blow it, this question haunts me: *Whatever possessed you to do such a thing?* And it should haunt me, because it keeps me honest and humble. But the good news is that regardless of how much I stumble, God is always there to catch me and set me

back on my feet again. I simply have to call out to him, whether
it is as simple as . . .

"Help me,"
"Forgive me,"
"I'm sorry,"

. . . or as complicated as a desperate outpouring of my soul. As
desperation leads to confession, it takes me through at least seven
phases:

Conviction: Admitting that what I said, did, or thought was
wrong.

Comprehension: Understanding the impact of my failures
and feeling genuine, heartfelt regret for how I have hurt God,
others, and myself.

Communication: Verbalizing my failure honestly to God
without justification, defensiveness, or blame.

Cleansing: Asking God to forgive me and give me a new
start.

Change: Determining that I will not repeat the failure and
setting up a plan to facilitate change.

Correction: Making any repairs or restitution to those I may
have wronged, thus reminding myself that sin hurts.

Celebration: Rejoicing at the chance to make a fresh start
and having a strong sense of gratitude and love toward God.

As Ruth Haley Barton wrote, "Let desperation do its good
work." David admitted, "Finally, I confessed all my sins to you and
stopped trying to hide my guilt. . . . And you forgave me!" (Psalm

32:5). Forgiveness shatters the chains of guilt and shame, allowing me to walk and run and dance. When my sins are forgiven, I'm free to celebrate and shout for joy at the top of my lungs. With the incredible and exciting freedom that comes through confession, I can pursue this journey with an exuberance I have never before experienced. With confession comes the beginning of good works.

So let the good works begin.

DAY 10

FACING REALITY

WE ALL HAVE WEAKNESSES AND FAILURES. That's just the way life is. So why do we try so hard to cover them up? The reality is that to be human is to be less than perfect—sometimes far less than perfect. The more we understand and accept our humanity, the more we will realize that we need to reach out to God. We *need* a Savior, because we desperately need to be saved.

Calvin Miller wrote, "Only when Christ comes in do we discover our own definition and why we are in the world. We are saved from living the undefined life." It is here that his light completes and guides and defines us.

To make any progress on this journey to an extraordinary faith, we have to start by facing facts. We must open our eyes to see our wounds and weaknesses in the brilliant light of God's glory and grandeur. In her book *Invitation to Solitude and Silence*, Ruth Haley Barton talks about the spiritual journey and explains that "waiting . . . is about becoming safe enough with God that we are no longer defending ourselves or hiding ourselves in his presence." The only way to feel this sort of safety is to face reality head-on with honesty, humility, and confession. Only after this desperate exposure and extreme vulnerability can we see God for who he really is.

Jeremiah was right when he wrote, "The human heart is the most deceitful of all things, and desperately wicked" (Jeremiah 17:9).

Nobody is perfect. We're all guilty. We all have problems. We're all broken. But God's grace is more than enough.

VERSE TO REMEMBER

Everyone has sinned; we all fall short of God's glorious standard.—ROMANS 3:23

QUESTIONS TO PONDER

+ What things in your own life do you need to get real about before you will be ready to truly risk faith?

+ What does it means to live the "undefined life"? How do you think God might bring definition to or even change the definition of your life?

+ How can embracing brokenness draw us closer to God's completeness?

QUOTE TO INSPIRE

When brokenness appears in our lives, openness appears in the heaven.—TOMMY TENNEY

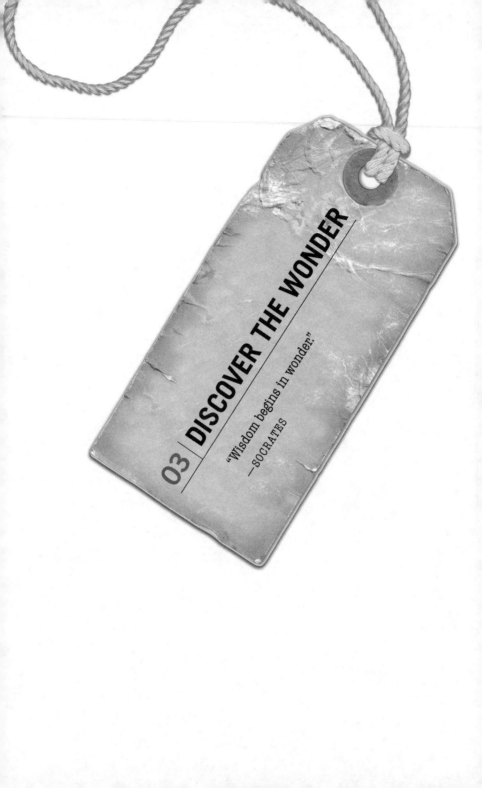

03 | DISCOVER THE WONDER

"Wisdom begins in wonder."
—SOCRATES

DAY 11

THE WONDER OF SEEING GOD

See God in everything, and God will calm and color all that thou dost see.—HANNAH WHITALL SMITH

EVERYTHING LOOKS DIFFERENT IN THE DARK.

With flashlights in hand, eight-year-old Dylan and I walked through the scrub pines and sagebrush of the high desert. We explored the shadows and strange shapes that appear when the darkness descends. Suddenly Dylan stopped.

I shone my flashlight on him.

"What's wrong?"

Dylan stood motionless before me, staring upward with his mouth open in amazement.

"Wow!"

That's all he said, but somehow that one word said it all. We were camping far from the city lights, and it was a crystal clear night. Dylan was totally transfixed by the spectacular display of sparkling stars that surrounded us. Once we looked up, we couldn't help but be drawn into the marvelous and miraculous. We were captivated and could not pull ourselves away.

"How many are there?" Dylan asked without moving.

"Too many to count."

"Wow!" he said again.

We stood there for the next ten minutes, silently staring upward, lost in wonder. On that night I saw the sky through the eyes of an eight-year-old and was reminded of what an incredible universe we live in.

One of the greatest obstacles to an extraordinary faith is our inability to see God—his character, his handiwork, his awesomeness—in everything. We are surrounded by wonders. The overwhelming reality of the spiritual world is waiting for all who are willing to slow down with open eyes and open hearts. God is always just before us, and his wonders press in on us at every turn. We don't need to look; we need to see.

We need to be willing to see God in all the people and places and things we would never think to look at. God is everywhere, and his mark is on everything, even those places and things that have been marred and degraded by human selfishness. What we all must grasp is that where God is, there will be wonder. As this sinks into our hearts, we will never see life and faith the same, for the two will become melded together in a remarkable way.

Every day is an adventure. Yet I think I've lost that sense of wonder. The amazement has faded, and I've outgrown that feeling of joyful astonishment. I've grown bored and boring, cold and complacent. I lead a practical life, based on what I do rather than what I see. I guess I just don't have the time or tenacity to seek his wonder and be taken aback, speechless and breathless, by his majesty and mystery.

Children frequently see what we don't. Brennan Manning, a former Franciscan priest and powerful author, wrote, "We have grown up. We no longer catch our breath at the sight of a rainbow or the scent of a rose, as we once did." An extraordinary faith sees God in the smallest and most ordinary things, as well as the grandest and most spectacular. Jesus commended childlike faith. As he was surrounded by children, he said that "the Kingdom of God belongs to those who are like these children" (Mark 10:14). C. S. Lewis insisted that children almost always see beyond the obvious to the "hidden story," while adults hardly ever do.

An old tale is told of a student who said to his teacher that each evening he saw an angel roll away the dark.

"Yes," said the teacher. "In my youth I saw angels too, but now that I have grown I no longer see such things."

I think we've all become a little jaded, narrow minded, and shortsighted. I am excellent at ignoring wonder, explaining away astonishment, and diminishing the value of anything real. If it doesn't make sense, it just doesn't seem real. Yet what if what is most real makes the least sense? Not because it is senseless or irrational, but because it lies beyond our limited senses and rationality.

Faith is the widening of our vision. Charles Swindoll, a bestselling author, wrote, "Vision encompasses vast vistas outside the realm of the predictable, the safe, and the expected." Yet within my limited vision, I see little beyond my own preconceived notions of normalcy.

In this age of information and communication, it's easy to lose our vision. But as a result of that lost vision, my soul has grown empty. Peter Kreeft, in *Everything You Ever Wanted to Know about Heaven*, wrote that in medieval times people were keenly aware of the awe and wonder that daily surrounded them in every conceivable form. The universe has not changed, but we have. "The universe has not become empty and we, full; it has remained full and we have become empty, insensitive to its fullness, cold hearted," wrote Kreeft. This emptiness steals everything that gives life real meaning. It also drains faith of all that makes it faith. For faith requires wonder to lift it above the ordinary and into a supernatural realm. And without the supernatural, genuine faith can't exist. If there were no wonder, there would be

+ no excitement
+ no joy
+ no awe
+ no amazement
+ no mystery
+ no miracles
+ no surprises
+ no salvation

I am ready for an extraordinary faith, and I know that in order to find this kind of faith, I must recapture a strong, exuberant sense of wonder. So as I walk through this world, I have to ask myself, *What makes my soul wonder?*

DAY 12

THE WONDER OF BEAUTY

God's fingers can touch nothing but to mold it into
loveliness.—GEORGE MACDONALD

GOD PLACES BEAUTY AT OUR FEET DAILY.

Yet most of the time I'm so busy and distracted that I fail to
recognize what is right in front of me. If I do behold beauty, it slips
too quickly from my memory as I move on to my next event.

My mind races back, remembering times of wonder in my own
life, each more beautiful than my clumsy words can capture:

+ an enormous full moon perfectly reflected on the dark blue
  surface of a smooth-as-glass lake
+ the sweet smell of honeysuckle on a warm summer day
+ the majesty of a family of deer grazing in a lush, green
  meadow
+ the hush of fresh snow falling gently onto roads and
  rooftops
+ a golden sun dropping slowly into the sea and splashing
  brilliant hues of red, orange, and pink onto the darkening sky

The Bible starts with, "In the beginning God created the heavens and the earth. . . . Then God looked over all he had made, and he saw that it was very good!" (Genesis 1:1, 31). God knew that his creation was incredible and elegant and beautiful. Saint Bernard of Clairvaux, a twelfth-century French monk, said, "I have seen but a fraction of God's glory, and it is awesome."

Nature offers us a slight glimpse of a glorious God. David wrote that "the heavens proclaim the glory of God" (Psalm 19:1). And the prophet Isaiah continued with, "The whole earth is filled with his glory!" (Isaiah 6:3).

There is wonder in anything glorious. Even the words associated with glory cause us to step back: *splendor, magnificence, grandeur, brilliance, radiance,* and *excellence.* These are power words that make us stop and ponder, reminding us not only of the greatness and beauty of nature but of God himself.

God is the source of all beauty. This universe is a reflection of who he is. As I explore and marvel at God's spectacular creation, I'm drawn closer to the wonder of God himself. Mallory Ortberg says it wonderfully: "God has woven himself irretrievably into Nature; left his fingerprints behind to show us where he's been. His signature is smeared into the curls of the Milky Way, forever circling above the rim of the world."

The human heart contains an unquenchable thirst for beauty. I'm drawn to it and astonished by it. Aristotle said that beauty is the "gift of God." Beauty stuns and surprises and lifts me upward. Beauty opens my eyes to the majesty of God. It becomes a stark contrast to my own brokenness and imperfection. The reality of this contrast causes me to yearn even more for God's glory. As Saint Augustine wrote in *Confessions,* "In my ugliness I plunged into the beauties you had made." I need beauty because I need God. His beauty is a reflection of all that is good and right within him. I long to join Moses when he said, "Let the beauty of the LORD our God be upon us" (Psalm 90:17, KJV).

The more I know God, the more aware I become of the beauty around me. I grow passionate about beauty in general and his beauty in particular, though I do not always know where one ends and the other begins. As Gabriela Mistral, a Chilean poet, wrote, "Love beauty; it is the shadow of God on the universe." For indeed his beauty is so big that it leaves me in awe and wonder of his limitless, awesome glory. His great and infinite beauty leaves me humble. It also opens my feeble eyes to the world around me. In this state of heightened awareness, I am able to see the supernatural through the natural. As Rebecca Manley Pippert wrote in *Hope Has Its Reasons*, "We find our senses are so heightened that the sky really seems bluer, the grass greener and every second charged with the grandeur of God."

Therefore let's appreciate the beauty God has made for us—absorb it, embrace it. Step outside this very moment and bathe in it. Study the sky and landscape with all its colors and contrasts. Listen to the birds, the wind, the water. Breathe in the scents of the flowers and trees, the fresh smells after a rain. Feel the sunshine on your face, the trunk of a tree under your fingertips, the ground beneath your bare feet. Isn't it amazing? As we do this every chance we get, we cannot help but live a life full to the brim with wonder.

As I write these words, I am overwhelmed by the beauty of God's creation. I am sitting beneath a grove of palm trees in Mexico, watching the waves of the ocean break onto the sandy shore. Each wave, with its steady strength, is different from the one before. A pelican skims across the water and dives deep for some invisible catch. The sky above me is brilliant blue, and the bougainvillea behind me is an almost phosphorescent red. I inhale the beauty, knowing that my paltry words are so grossly inadequate.

My mind wanders back to my home in Oregon, where just a week ago I enjoyed a totally different type of beauty as the first fall frost left a crisp white coating on the grass and pumpkins. Meanwhile the trees blazed bright as their leaves turned orange. A woodpecker tapped its beak into a rotten snag with rapid-fire determination, while a bushy-tailed squirrel raced to and fro in search of food to keep him cozy through the upcoming winter.

God has an awesome imagination. My experiences in Mexico and Oregon represent such different aspects of his beauty, yet they are only small glimpses into the infinite canvases, in this world and beyond, upon which he displays his works and wonders.

From now on, I'm going to strive to find wonder in every nook and cranny of this everyday world. And once I find it, I plan to savor it with all my senses and never let it go.

DAY 13

THE WONDER OF MYSTERY AND MIRACLES

At its very core, life is . . . a mystery in the best sense of the term—an engaging, thrilling, and deliberate mystery.

—RAVI ZACHARIAS

MYSTERY SURROUNDS US.

There is so much I do not understand about life and death, love and pain, people and nature, triumph and tragedy, heaven and hell. The list is endless. Yet mystery often makes me feel uncomfortable and out of control. So in an attempt to order my life, I try to ignore or explain away the mystery. I create beliefs and formulas and judgments that make the world more understandable. But all my arguments and theories do not change the fact that I am still faced with mysteries every day—incredible, mind-boggling mysteries. Rather than resist them, why not marvel in their wonder and let them be a part of my journey?

Mysteries are matters of faith, not reason. Reason has limits, but faith has no limits. Therefore, mystery is the stuff that faith is made of. It is built on amazing dreams that defy explanation, expand imagination, and create a reality that is more real than our mere five senses can validate. As David Benner wrote in *Sacred Companions*, "A spiritual journey that seeks to eliminate all that is mysterious will never take us far enough from our comfort zone for genuine transformation."

Life is full of shadows and fog. As a teenager I would lie restlessly on my bed and struggle with questions like, *How long is eternity?* and *How far is infinity?* I concentrated on these challenges until I was so frustrated that my head hurt. Lately, however, I've been trying to relax with these mysteries and stop struggling to figure them out. I can now marvel at them because I don't need to master them.

God's call is not an invitation *out* of the unknown; rather, he wants his people to step deeper *into* it. For the deeper we travel into the mystery, the greater our trust must be and the more worthless ordinary faith becomes.

Mystery pulls me out of the mind-numbing monotony and apathy that can so easily overwhelm me. I've found that once I relax with the mysterious, it is the most exciting and beautiful thing I can experience. It is only then that I realize how desperately I need more moments of mysterious wonder. It is as if I am curiously gazing into the crystal waters of a bottomless pond. My brain struggles to solve the mystery, but my soul smiles at it. Matthew Henry, a seventeenth-century English clergyman, instructs that when we cannot find the bottom, we must sit down at the brink and adore the depth. Only in the bottomless depth does life get really interesting.

We all have a longing for the mysterious—for things beyond this world. The mystery of God is at once attractive and unsettling, awesome and awful. To live by mystery we don't need to understand everything we experience, inwardly or outwardly. We might explore the mysterious by seeking, observing, studying, and asking, but if the answers are not apparent, we need not become angry or anxious or arrogant. Once we embrace mystery, we'll find peace and enchantment.

Mystery makes the supernatural real. It makes everything I experience richer, deeper, and truer. Mystery forces my faith to be what it was meant to be: extraordinary, unexplainable, supernatural. It allows God to be in control and not me, leaving me free to simply trust him and, like Julian of Norwich, to "be content whether he conceals or reveals."

I've come to see that every moment is an opportunity—regardless of how fearful I might be—to totally trust him as he carries me deeper into the depths of his mystery. Yet I know I'm still only a beginner in this wondrous journey.

As David Needham wrote in *Close to His Majesty*, "We are still at the edge of mystery. Dare we imagine what lies ahead of us as we climb higher and see further into the greatness, the wonder of this magnificent God?"

The wonder of the miraculous transports me into another realm where I no longer see life and everything it contains in the same manner as I once did. Something happens when I catch a glimpse of God—everything becomes new and different. The fabric of the universe grows thin, and I see something radiant and spectacular shining through it. Everywhere I look, the world is alive and ablaze with a glory that leaves me in a constant state of wonder. I know I will never be the same.

Donald Miller, in *Blue like Jazz*, wrote that "you cannot be a Christian without being a mystic." Mystics do not escape everything that surrounds them; in fact, they are intensely aware of mystery in the greatness and smallness of life. They humbly accept mystery in the face of reality.

In the essay *Why I Believe in Christianity*, G. K. Chesterton wrote, "The Christian . . . puts the contradiction into his philosophy. That mystery by its darkness enlightens all things." Mystery adds depth and light to our ordinary days. In the same essay, G. K. Chesterton said, "It is only the mystic, the man who accepts the contradictions, who can laugh and walk easily through the world."

This spectacular journey is not only mysterious, it is also miraculous. Terry Hershey encourages us to "create a fabric in our soul which absorbs daily miracles." Yet I know that sometimes my hurry and superficiality blind me to the miracles that surround me. I only see the bright lights and broad strokes of life, completely overlooking the subtle shadings and tender details that fill my days with amazing meaning that should, if I'm aware, take my breath away. Living a miraculous life means walking in and out of the daily doldrums, having faith that God will guide, protect, and see us through. It also is a willingness and receptiveness to God's presence wherever we might be. Erwin McManus wrote, "However mundane a moment may appear, the miraculous may wait to be unwrapped within it."

Miracles don't always explode above our heads in spectacular fireworks. Sometimes they quietly visit in practical, everyday, almost mundane forms. Yet they are still miracles.

I was hiking through a wilderness area in southern Oregon on a hot August afternoon with my then two-year-old daughter on my shoulders. It was a beautiful day, and I was marveling at God's handiwork. As I stepped over a log, Brittany grabbed my head to keep her balance, and one of her tiny fingers slipped into my eye. I was wearing hard contact lenses and one popped out of my eye onto the rocky ground. For the next hour I crawled on my hands and knees, carefully searching every square inch of where it might have fallen. The contact had disappeared, and I had no replacement.

That night I had a dream that God was speaking to me. He asked why I had not spoken to him about my lost contact. He said, "If you had come to me, I would have shown you where it is." I replied, "God, I'm sorry I didn't come to you. But here I am, if it's not too late."

Suddenly my dream shifted and I saw a stone about the size of my fist with a small amount of moss on it. The stone was at the side of a path near a large fir tree. As I looked, I saw a small crevice between the mossy stone and another stone. In the crevice I saw my contact lens sparkling in the sun. Then I awoke. *What a strange dream!*

Early the next morning I hiked to the place I had lost my contact. I went to the large fir tree. I looked down and saw the stone with the moss. I bent down and stared into the small crevice on the left side of the stone. There was my contact, sparkling in the sun. At first I couldn't believe it! Had God really told me where to look? Maybe he had. Or maybe it was just a coincidence, good luck, or a freak accident.

Why is it so hard for me to admit this might have been a miracle?

I think it's because we are just not accustomed to miracles. In fact, we are trained to overlook and explain away mysteries and miracles. These do not fit within a mind-set that insists we are the center of the universe. Mysteries and miracles remind us that there is something greater and smarter and more powerful than us, so we fight the miraculous and believe we must solve the mysterious.

But miracles are simply God's way of arousing awe and wonder, of making sure we do not forget who he is. Miracles keep life exciting, whether they are as small as a twinkle in a baby's eye or as large as a hundred million worlds orbiting a million suns in a midnight sky. Miracles shine the spotlight on the supernatural in the midst of everyday life.

Willa Cather, an American novelist, wrote, "Miracles . . . seem to me to rest not so much upon faces or voices or healing power coming suddenly near to us from afar off, but upon our perceptions being made finer, so that for a moment our eyes can see and our ears can hear what is there about us always."

From now on, I plan to keep my soul open, ready, and expectant, for at any moment a single miracle, or possibly a cascade of miracles, just might descend upon me.

I am looking forward to that moment.

DAY 14

THE WONDER OF PUZZLES AND PARADOX

> As we come into a greater sense of what we don't know,
> our appreciation of how awesome God is increases
> because we have to trust. —RICHARD HANSON

SOMETIMES THINGS JUST DON'T MAKE ANY SENSE.

These are times I feel frustrated or uneasy. I like it when everything goes smoothly, with no confusion or complication. I like it when things fit into neat little boxes. Yet this is not how life usually goes. Every day I run into experiences that are perplexing, difficult, or downright impossible to comprehend. There are no pat answers or straightforward formulas when it comes to extraordinary faith.

Life is a puzzle—and it's not a straight-edged, single-sided puzzle with a few thousand pieces. Instead, life is a double-sided puzzle with irregular boundaries and unlimited pieces.

Sometimes when I'm doing a puzzle, I can't find the right pieces; they don't even seem to be on the table. So I have several choices: force the pieces, try harder, or accept the puzzle for what it is. I've been known to force certain pieces to make them fit, and I even try to convince myself that they fit, but in reality I know that they just aren't supposed to go in that place.

Puzzles are designed to be *puzzling*. And so are life's puzzles. They stretch us and remind us that life is much more complex than we think, filled with paradoxes and hidden meanings that keep us constantly on the edge of our seats.

A paradox is a puzzle, and to me, a puzzle is something to be solved. I need to figure it out. I need a reasonable explanation. I need an answer to every question, but my answers are usually incomplete and generate even more questions.

God seems to like paradox. He loves to turn certainty and conventions upside down. The word *paradox* literally means "beyond belief" or "unbelievable." It describes circumstances in which two opposing, and seemingly contradictory, facts are held in tension. Most people believe that either one or the other fact must be truth, but in a supernatural realm, opposing facts can actually be true at the same time.

+ God is one person and he is three.
+ Jesus is fully human and fully divine.
+ God is in total control and we have complete responsibility.
+ Faith is an unearned gift and we must seek it.
+ God chooses us to freely choose him.
+ God is the beginning and the end of an infinite universe.

Each of these statements holds two truths that appear to be in conflict. Our rational minds say that one of these truths must be in error or at least not as fully true as the other. We go through all sorts of mental gymnastics in order to make our beliefs logical and consistent and tidy. Yet if we are totally honest, no matter how brilliant, creative, or elegant our solutions, there is always that stubborn piece that just won't fit.

Is it possible to live and grow and journey onward without all the answers?

What if questions, not answers, are the building blocks of the universe?

What if the answers actually get in the way, allowing us to trust in our own cleverness and logic and understanding rather than in God?

What if the answers keep us from fully trusting God?

What if they create a perceptual filter that keeps us from truly seeing who he is and hearing what he so desperately wants to say to us?

Paradox is not a contradiction of reality; it is only a contradiction of what I believed reality to be. We look at a paradox, scratch our heads, and say, "This cannot be!" But the fact that paradox throws us off balance doesn't mean that balance does not exist. Paradox stretches what we thought was true, but it doesn't disregard it.

Paradox propels us into wonder and a supernatural level of enlightenment. It's a fulfillment and completion of the picture. Because of this Leonard Sweet, a postmodern theologian, says, "Christianity pivots on paradox." There will come a day when we look at those paradoxes that perplexed us so and say, "Why was I so blind? There is no difficulty here." For at that point we will realize that paradoxes are mere riddles meant to pull us deeper into our faith and closer to our mysterious, infinite God.

Paradox is a wonderful, fulfilling, exciting part of our faith. Carolyn Arends wrote in *Living the Questions*, "When I encounter a paradox, I know I've come across a chance to get a tiny glimpse of the *blaze* and the *blur* that illuminates and clarifies all truth. I've found a keyhole to the Divine." This keyhole surprises me because until I look through it, I have no idea how dim my vision has been and how limited my understanding still is.

I know so little compared to a God who knows so much. Yet ordinary faith elevates knowledge and the search for knowledge to a point that leaves no room for real, risky faith. We believe we must know it all. Facts have replaced faith. But I've realized it's okay that I don't know everything and that much of what I do know I don't understand.

I have no choice but to live with gaps and questions, conflicts and inconsistencies, riddles and conundrums. I need to piece together what I can of the puzzles and make peace with the paradox.

The fact that so many of God's ways are paradoxical and hidden to human reason drove the prophet Isaiah to proclaim, "Truly you are a God who hides himself" (Isaiah 45:15, NIV). Yet here is another paradox, for the God who hides encourages us to seek him. He yearns to be found. Living with and in paradox is not a passive behavior. It must be woven deep into the fabric of daily life, even though it may run against the pattern. The principles are clear:

1. Give, so you will receive.
2. Die to self, so you will live.
3. Be silent, so you will speak wisely.
4. Be last, so you will be first.
5. Wait, so you will move forward.
6. Surrender, so you will have victory.
7. Accept weakness, so you will be strong.
8. Flee temptation, so you will stand firm.
9. Fight, so you will have peace.

10.   Suffer, so you will celebrate.
11.   Forgive, so you will be forgiven.
12.   Be childlike, so you will be mature.

Paradox doesn't have to make sense, but those who relax with it and live it find that it works. There is a freedom that comes when I let go of trying to figure everything out and trust God with the puzzles and paradoxes of life.

Paul Tournier, a Swiss psychiatrist, wrote, "Faith is not shelter against difficulties, but belief in the face of all contradictions." Let's go one step further and say that faith is belief in the face of *anything*. Let's also accept that there is wonder in everything. Complete understanding takes away the awe.

On this mysterious journey, I must risk the mystery. After all, I don't need to know the answers. I just need to believe that God does.

DAY 15

THE WONDER OF SURPRISE

We live by God's surprises.—HELMUT THIELICKE

SURPRISES ARE THE SALT AND PEPPER OF LIFE.

God is consistent and dependable and full of surprises. Once I think I have him figured out, he pulls a fast one on me. He leaps out of the shadows, catches me off guard, and winks knowingly at me. He shows up where he is least expected, leaving his fingerprints of wonder—joy, beauty, peace, victory, mystery—anywhere and everywhere.

Yet in this hurried and hectic world, I have little time for surprises. They interrupt my carefully planned schedule, throwing things into chaos. My life is structured and organized, with far too many obligations, responsibilities, appointments, and deadlines. There's little room for free time. Even if God tried to jump in and catch my attention, I wonder if I would notice. I think it's time for a change.

Oswald Chambers, a Scottish devotional writer in the early twentieth century, wrote, "[God] packs our life with surprises all the time." God may be hidden, but he does not hide. He embeds hundreds of hints and innuendos into each day and then waits patiently for us to find him—to open our eyes and ears and hearts to discover what C. S. Lewis called a "deeper magic." These are surprises with a purpose. Sometimes they leave me dazed and dizzy, but they always remind me that God is amazing beyond my wildest imagination. It may be a patch of blue sky on a cloudy day when I need encouragement or a cross on a hillside when I need a reminder that God is near.

When I was in my early twenties, I was nearly engaged to a wonderful girl I was dating at the time. But strange, seemingly random events forced us to break up. I was so surprised, and I cried out to God, "What in the world are you doing?" I had thought God was opening doors and leading one way, but suddenly those doors were slammed shut and I was being led in a totally different direction.

I was confused, lonely, discouraged, and perplexed. Love and relationships seemed to be such a mystery, but what God was doing in my life seemed like an even greater mystery. I was tired of the games and frustrations of relationships, yet I also felt incomplete without someone to share my life with. I struggled with what to do and finally decided to simply do nothing. If God wanted me in a relationship, he would have to provide one. I shared these thoughts with my good friend Tami, and she told me she felt the same way. Over the next few months, we would often meet at the local Dairy Queen, talking for hours about the pitfalls of relationships and trying to encourage each other.

I had known Tami and her family for a long time. She was sweet and smart and had a beautiful smile. We could talk about anything, although never in my wildest dreams had I ever thought about dating Tami. We were just friends. But then it hit me: We *were* dating. It didn't take long for us to fall in love and get married.

What a surprise! Through all my ups and downs with relationships, Tami had been there, right under my nose. Yet God waited for the perfect time to open my eyes to this wonderful surprise. Every day God orchestrates millions of details into an amazing symphony of life. Even when the individual notes seem sharp or disjointed, he fits them together in surprisingly powerful and beautiful ways. Certainly there are painful parts of our lives that may not make sense to us in this lifetime. But somehow God can bring ultimate good out of even the most difficult circumstances.

I think God loves to surprise us with his greatness. He is so much more than we ever expected. In my journey to interpret and understand God, I end up limiting him and making him much too small. I label him and box him in, making him predictable and familiar and safe. I reduce him to what my perceptual and intellectual abilities can grasp.

Yet this is just a glimpse of God. Labels make no difference to him, and definitions can never adequately define him. He is beyond mere words and cleverly crafted boxes. He wants to stretch our comfortable categories, surprising us at every turn. Sometimes he's a Baptist, a Lutheran, or Orthodox; other times he's a Catholic, a Pentecostal, or a Methodist. At different times he's a liberal, a conservative, or a moderate; he may also be a Republican, a Democrat, or an Independent.

Yet there is also a shape and order to God. He lets us know that he is light and life and love. He reveals that he is personal and infinite, tender and all powerful, timely and eternal. He is a wonderful, brilliant mix of surprises whom we can draw near to but never quite catch. Yet he still encourages us to try, warning us to trust him and to "not depend on your own understanding" (Proverbs 3:5).

If I ever hope to grow and thrive, I must leave room for the unexpected. His surprises keep me alert and constantly aware that life is not under my control. G. K. Chesterton reminds us that "this world is a wild and startling place." I simply need to open my eyes and pay attention. And when I do, God's surprises stun me and shock me and leave me speechless. They are impossible and impressive and unexpected. They fill me with unbelievable wonder. A God surprise might include:

+ a stairway to heaven
+ a burning bush
+ a sea dividing to make a path
+ a talking donkey
+ a giant killed by a boy with a slingshot
+ a jug of oil that never runs dry
+ a den of hungry lions that don't attack
+ the Son of God being born in a manger

And these are just the beginnings of God's surprises. Every day a new and different surprise is waiting for each one of us. It may be a remarkable solution to a difficult problem, an amazing rescue from a dangerous situation, or an undeniable answer to an impossible prayer. For me it is often nature's incredible beauty or finding the perfect words at just the right time. The wonderful thing about an extraordinary faith is that the surprises never end.

DAY 16

HOW WONDERFUL!

THIS WORLD OVERFLOWS with wonders of every kind—holy wonders, dangerous wonders, enchanting wonders, sensational wonders, reassuring wonders, incomprehensible wonders. God has miraculously infused every moment and experience, every object and person, with some form of wonder.

To ignore wonder is to ignore God. For wonder is what draws us to God and opens our eyes to who he really is—his goodness and glory and grace. Yet the wonders of this limited world are nothing compared to those of the world to come.

In the summertime of 593 BC, Ezekiel discovered the wonder. At the age of thirty, while standing beside a river in ancient Babylon, he felt the hand of God take hold of him. Before he could move he saw things that could only be described as mysterious, paradoxical, and surprising. What he saw was beyond words, but it burned amazing images on his mind. What he saw was like . . .

+ gleaming amber
+ burnished bronze
+ bright coals
+ brilliant torches
+ flashes of lightning
+ sparkling crystal
+ flickering fire
+ radiant rainbows

The wonder was so great that Ezekiel fell facedown in the dirt. He didn't move until God told him to stand back up. On that day, Ezekiel started his mysterious journey, and he would never be the same again. He could no longer be satisfied with an ordinary faith; he had faced the wonder and seen a glimpse of God. From this point on, there was no turning back.

VERSE TO REMEMBER

When you came down long ago, you did awesome deeds beyond our highest expectations. And oh, how the mountains quaked!—ISAIAH 64:3

QUESTIONS TO PONDER

+ When we miss or grow cool to all the marvels that surround us, we diminish ourselves at every level. How does a lack of wonder affect you:
    intellectually?
    emotionally?
    physically?

socially?

spiritually?

+ As children, we are all born with a sense of wonder. What memories do you have of your own childlike wonder? What can you do to recapture some of that awe and mystery?

+ How does a sense of wonder draw people closer to God?

QUOTE TO INSPIRE

The moment one gives close attention to anything, even a blade of grass, it becomes a mysterious, awesome, indescribably magnificent world in itself.—HENRY MILLER

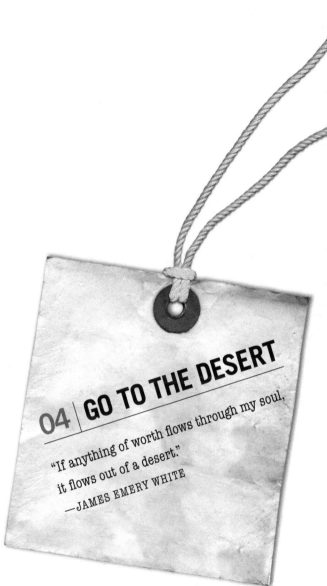

04 | GO TO THE DESERT

"If anything of worth flows through my soul,
it flows out of a desert."
—JAMES EMERY WHITE

DAY 17

GOD'S COUNTRY

In the empty desert, the spirit transforms.

—PAMELA REEVE

MY GRANDFATHER LOVED THE DESERT.

As a kid I couldn't understand what he saw in such an ugly place. I figured that when you get old you must get a little crazy. His favorite desert place was Christmas Valley in southeastern Oregon. He showed me pictures of it, and I was not impressed. It was flat and empty and dry, but Grandpa thought it was one of the most beautiful places in the world.

A few years ago I decided to go to Christmas Valley to see if I could discover its secret power over Grandpa. It was 105 degrees as I drove into this tiny, isolated desert community about a hundred miles from any significant city. I drove past a few small buildings and went sixteen miles farther into nothing. Then I turned off the two-lane highway and went three or four miles deeper into the desert on a dusty, unpaved, single-lane road. I stopped my car and stepped into the heat. I looked around: sand, sagebrush, and blue sky.

I stood there, scanning the horizon as the sun beat down on

me. The landscape of the desert was stark. It was wide open and monotonous. This place was different from anyplace else I had ever been. The desert was harsh, and it made no apologies. There seemed to be a brutal honesty here; I had no place to hide. There was also simplicity here, and in that simplicity there was beauty.

Grandpa was right.

I continued to look for something, but I didn't know what it was. There was nothing there, nothing to do or see or hear. It was a desolate place, bleak and barren. After a short while I was ready to move on, but for some reason I stayed. There was mystery in the desert, and I wanted to figure it out. I refused to let this wilderness beat me.

The sun pounded down on my head, and I wished I had brought a hat. I looked for shade but there was none, so I sat down on a rock to relax and regroup. It was hard and uncomfortable. The heat sapped my energy, and the dryness parched my throat. I drank the last two swallows from my water bottle and set it against the rock. The sweat dripped down the side of my face, and I just let it drip. Someone once said that the desert is as brilliant as it is hard. So where was the brilliance?

In the early years of Christianity, hundreds of people went to the desert and encouraged others to follow them. Their call was simple: "Go to the desert, and it will teach you everything you need to know." In biblical times some of the greatest people of faith went to the desert: Moses, David, Elijah, John the Baptist, and even Jesus. The desert is uncluttered, and in it are few distractions. It is a wilderness that is both dangerous and wonderful. It's the real world, stripped down and exposed, and it left me breathless.

In the desert, I felt vulnerable. I was removed from people, activity, and distraction; it was just God and me, nobody else.

All my defenses were peeled away, and I was exposed to the elements—wind, dust, lack of water, wild animals, and extreme heat with little shade. Anyone who saw me in this environment might have assumed I was in control, but I wasn't.

I could see that the desert could be a strict teacher. In the desert, we have no choice but to live by its rules; it takes us to the basics. The desert can be enlightening, as it renews the mind and rejuvenates the heart.

It is in the desert that we find God, and in finding God we find ourselves. Or maybe we find ourselves and then find that we cannot live meaningfully without God. In his book *The Healing Path*, Dan Allender wrote, "The desert shatters the soul's arrogance and leaves body and soul crying out in thirst and hunger. In the desert, we trust God or we die."

As I stood by that rock in Christmas Valley with sweat running down my neck, I finally got it. The very thing that had caused me to disregard the desert was what made it most valuable. Its emptiness allowed God to fill it with his meaning. Three life-changing gifts come from this desert emptiness.

Solitude: No one was around for miles and miles, except a car passing in the distance every fifteen or twenty minutes.
Stillness: Nothing moved except the wind through the sagebrush and a hawk circling overhead.
Silence: There was a haunting, total quiet, except my own breathing and footsteps in the sandy soil.

Without these three gifts, our faith stays tethered to everyday life. This world is full of crowds, hurry, and nonstop noise, and the soul cannot grow in such an environment. It is left stunted and ordinary, not to mention empty and worn out. To move beyond the superficial, I think we must find our desert and go to it frequently.

Grandpa had learned the lessons of the desert, and I finally understood what he meant when he said that Christmas Valley was "God's country."

DAY 18

SOLITUDE

No one can approach God without withdrawing from
the world. —SAINT ISAAC OF SYRIA

SOMETIMES PEOPLE DRIVE ME CRAZY.

I spend much of my days with people—teaching, counseling,
encouraging, socializing, playing, or just hanging out—and most
of the time I love it. People amaze and intrigue me; each person
has a unique story. Every day people teach me and challenge me
and inspire me. Yet after a certain amount of time, I just need to
escape. Too many people for too long makes my soul troubled. I
hit a certain point when I need to break free and get away from
it all—to renew, refresh, and rejuvenate myself. Even when the
people around me are the most intelligent, creative, loving, wonderful, motivating people, I still get that feeling.

Sometimes when I'm surrounded by too many people, it messes
with my focus and faith. Crowds can be overwhelming. They
bring out the very worst in me—all that is petty and proud. Other
times, crowds make me driven, defensive, or distracted, pulling
me in a direction completely opposite of where I really want to

go. They tighten their grip and tug at my soul, even as I try to resist. These people are not necessarily evil in their intentions. It's just that their dramas and dogmas take me places that don't satisfy my soul.

It always seems there are people pressing in on me. I have to fight for moments of solitude. If I don't, I grow impatient, scattered, and shallow. I've always known that I need to care for my soul in this way. As a kid, I would hide in my fort beneath the stairs and look through my comic books by the bright glare of a bare lightbulb hanging from the ceiling. As a college student I would retreat to a cozy alcove on the second floor of Smith Hall, where I could stretch out on the worn-out couch and study without interruption. As an adult with a houseful of kids, it's sometimes more difficult to find my needed solitude. Yet periodically I'll dodge into my bedroom or den, where I'll catch my breath with a book or the Bible.

Now don't get me wrong: I strongly believe that we need people. We all have a social side that needs others to help us grow. Without people, it's easy to become isolated and indifferent. People provide company and comfort, perspective and protection, encouragement and accountability. It is healthy for us to reach out to others and allow others to reach out to us. We need both: moments of community and moments of seclusion.

Solomon reminded us that there is "a time to embrace and a time to turn away" (Ecclesiastes 3:5). Embracing provides connection. Turning away, when it is not done in anger or despondency, provides space for the soul to stretch broader and deeper and closer to God.

When my days get out of control, I dream of a simpler place and time. I yearn for a peaceful spot beyond the pressure and propaganda of my current life. I would love to escape to a solitary desert far away from the influence and intoxication of the bright lights. The desert is a place of rest and a chance to regroup, away from crowds and confusion. Few people gather or live in the desert. The only people you actually meet there are those who are passing through, usually as quickly as possible, or those who are seeking a place to escape.

Even Jesus needed to escape the crowds and get away for a while. The Gospel of Matthew says, "He left in a boat to a remote area to be alone" (Matthew 14:13). The Gospel of Mark says he went to "a quiet place" (Mark 6:32) or "a solitary place" (NIV). If Jesus needed his solitude, how much more do we need it?

Something about the monastic life sounds very appealing to me. I'd love to pack my bags and disappear from all the clutter of culture. I'd like to hide away deep in a desert, high on a mountain retreat, or even out on an isolated island. I often dream of these sorts of escapes where I could spend my days surrounded by uncommon simplicity—absorbing the wonders of nature, working with my hands, reflecting on life, meditating on God. Away from the craziness and commotion of everyday life, I could ponder and pray, read and journal, savor and enjoy each moment.

Yet solitude should not be too permanent a state. Even though solitude is important, it should be periodic and temporary. I retreat in order to return in a better state than when I left. I withdraw to gain a more winsome spirit and soul. Solitude strengthens and stabilizes me so that when I reenter community I am more patient, sensitive, and compassionate.

Solitude is crucial to faith. It allows me to step outside this world and into the supernatural. In solitude I come face-to-face with the basics:

1. God's greatness and glory
2. my own frailty, desperation, and dependence on him
3. the wonder of his willingness to communicate and care for me

Solitude provides an accurate picture of reality without all the smoke and mirrors. Solitude brings me inward—to think and feel and pray. This inwardness is not self-absorbed, for without others to impress, manipulate, or control, I am forced to face reality. As Calvin Miller wrote, "Inwardness draws us to that unseen reality. . . . Inwardness is the place where the believer and his Lord meet."

Solitude is an opportunity to wash away the ways of the world and simply become filled with God's presence. It's not just being alone; it is being alone with God. Solitude makes me more aware of my weaknesses and vulnerability as I stand alone—totally alone—before God. No one accompanies me or encourages me; no one protects or defends me. There are no crowds to blend into. I am fully exposed and naked as I deal with God one-on-one. It can be really frightening. Yet as Solomon wrote, "Fear of the LORD is the foundation of true knowledge" (Proverbs 1:7). After all, he is Lord of the desert.

In the desert of solitude, I am transformed. There I find a wilderness where his presence is formidable, a refuge where his protection is humbling, and a sanctuary where his holiness is purifying. As I learn to let go of all that traps me in the brokenness of this world—the frustrations, the worries, the stuff—I begin to experience peace and freedom that transform my faith from ordinary to extraordinary.

When I am surrounded by solitude, I can finally be myself and relax with God. The pressures and pretense of society fall away, and I am able to see God more clearly than before. Alone in the desert, I can better understand how Moses must have felt when he found God in a bush that burned but was not consumed.

I stop to marvel and reflect on mystery and paradox.

I see God in a flame.

I hear his voice.

I take off my shoes.

The desert doesn't allow its visitors to stay the same. It threatens all who enter, cutting them to the quick and watching them bleed. This is not always comfortable, but it is good. For through this, we are transformed. Saint Francis de Sales, a sixteenth-century French bishop, encouraged us to "retire at various times into the solitude of your own heart" and while there "converse heart to heart with God on your state of soul." Only then do our successes and failures lose their control over us, and we realize that much of what we thought was so important has relatively no importance at all. In the desert, our aloneness can swallow all we thought we were. Henri Nouwen, a Dutch priest and professor, wrote, "To live a spiritual life we must first find the courage to enter the desert of our loneliness and to change it by gentle and persistent efforts into a garden of solitude." In so doing we discover that our aloneness fulfills us by forcing us to shed the old life and discover something entirely new.

Solitude can happen anywhere—a bench in your backyard, a quiet room in your home, a spot at the seashore, a walk in the mountains. To me, nothing is more peaceful and relaxing than sitting on the bank of a stream. The sound of the water calms my spirit. Yet solitude is not a place; it's a frame of mind. The desert opens my heart, for when I am most thirsty I am most ready to drink, when I am most weary I am most open to help, and when I am most alone I am most willing to face the depth of my neediness. In solitude:

+ Distractions are abandoned.
+ Truth is pondered.
+ Deceptions are exposed.
+ Priorities are evaluated.
+ Humility is learned.
+ Purpose is discovered.
+ Peace is embraced.
+ Faith is deepened.

As I go to my desert, I think of Ruth Haley Barton's description of solitude as "an invitation to enter more deeply into the intimacy of relationship with the One who waits just outside the noise and busyness of our lives."

DAY 19

STILLNESS

At the still point, there the dance is.—T. S. ELIOT

IT'S 6:30 A.M. THANKSGIVING MORNING, and dawn is nearly ready to break. Everybody in my family is fast asleep, even Tami, as she lies quietly beside me. I wish I could just relax, roll over, and go back to sleep. But my body is restless and my mind is racing a hundred miles an hour. My mind is a demanding fellow. He's scheduling out the day and reminding me of all the things I need to do. He's planning out the chapter I'm writing and problem solving an issue at work and worrying about my kids and contemplating an upcoming meeting at church and considering what would be the most meaningful gift to get Tami for Christmas and . . . *Oh, stop it! This is insane!*

I lie still for another fifteen minutes, but my mind won't slow down. Finally I can't take it anymore, so I climb out of bed, shower, and tackle a project. Something deep inside drives me to constantly keep busy. Yet I know that we all need breaks in our days to breathe deeply and do nothing—time to calm down, slow down, and be still. I tend to move too much and too fast, basing my value on what I accomplish. The more I accomplish, the better I feel about myself. If I don't do enough or do it well enough or even do it quickly enough, I feel as if I have failed. I am constantly on the go, always doing *something*—even if that something has no real value or ultimate meaning.

In this go-as-fast-as-you-can world, it is hard to slow down.

In the 1947 movie classic *The Bishop's Wife*, Sylvester the cab-driver observes, "The main trouble is there are too many people who don't know where they're going and they want to get there too fast." At times this feels like a perfect description of my life. I really want to slow down, but it sure doesn't come easily. I love the excitement and energy of speed. If I slow down, I feel guilty. I want to be efficient and not waste time, so I move through life at such a fast pace that everything's a blur and I seem to be constantly catching my breath.

I must remind myself: I don't always have to be doing something. But even as I think those words, I'm restlessly looking for something to do. I feel so conflicted—until I get away and escape to my desert.

The desert forces me not only to slow down but to stand still. David wrote, "I have calmed and quieted myself" (Psalm 131:2). As I grow still, I begin to see epiphanies of:

+ who God is
+ how God works
+ what God does
+ why God matters

The faster I go, the more likely I am to miss God. In stillness, I am able to glimpse the supernatural in all its glory.

In today's world, I don't think we know how to slow down. Our schedules are full, but our lives are empty. We don't even have time to breathe. I mean really breathe—deep, full breaths that refresh us with a feeling of life and clarity. We stay on the move all day long, until we finally fall exhausted into our beds at night. Then the next morning we wake up to do it all over again. We wear ourselves out and then ask, *Where is the joy? Where is the excitement? Where is the fulfillment of life?*

I've found that the faster I go, the more apt I am to only skim the surface. And in doing so, I become shallow and superficial. I might get things done and look good, but it's only a facade. I can't possibly go deeper until I slow down, stay still, and pay attention. When I'm still, I see more, hear more, feel more, consider more, learn more, love more, and change more. I plumb the depths of meaning and maturity, courage and calmness, life and faith.

As a child, I was often told to stand still, but I couldn't. I thought being still sounded boring and inefficient. I had things to do and places to go. I didn't have the time to be still, at least not for long. Now that I'm an adult, I realize that I can actually accomplish more in my stillness than in all my rushing around. I need to learn to do less and be more, for this is where the care of my soul really happens. This is where I reconnect with myself.

Trappist monk Thomas Merton wrote that solitude and stillness help us "recuperate spiritual powers that may have been gravely damaged by the noise and rush of a pressurized existence."

So here I am, fourteen hours later on Thanksgiving Day, and I am finally slowing down. The house is still and so am I. Tami and the kids are still at her parents' house, but I snuck out early to get a little time alone. It has been a busy day with both sides of the family. We visited, laughed, told stories, played games, and ate more than we should have. And now I'm sitting in a large overstuffed chair in my family room enjoying some stillness and solitude.

I didn't turn on the TV, CD player, or computer. And I haven't even listened to the messages on the answering machine. There's a fire in the fireplace, and I'm enjoying simply staring into the flames.

I just sit still and be.

I reflect on God's greatness and grace, along with his love and lessons. I have so much to be thankful for—family, friends, faith—and that's just the beginning. It's sad that there is only one Thanksgiving Day each year. It would be good for me to set aside a day of thanks on a regular basis just to help me develop a more grateful heart.

A peace overwhelms me as the late night shadows surround me. I revel in the flickering stillness. Forty-five minutes pass, and my restlessness begins to return. As much as I know the healing power of stillness, I still find it really tough to *be* and not *do*. Something stirs my heart, and I feel driven to do something, anything. So I grab a pencil, pick up my notebook, and finish this chapter.

I wish the world operated on my timetable.

I like to plan out when things should happen, and I get terribly frustrated when people mess up my schedule. I don't like to be still and wait. It makes me nervous. I tap my foot, look at my watch, wonder what's happening, look at my watch again, pace the floor. All the while, I'm asking myself, *Why can't they hurry up?*

It takes patience to be still, and it takes even more to wait. David wrote, "Be still in the presence of the LORD, and wait patiently for him to act" (Psalm 37:7). Being still and waiting are acts of faith.

They require us to give up control and the insistence that God work on our timetables. They mean trusting that God has things under control—his control.

God may be silent, but we know he is there. And his silence forces us to be still and wait. The prophet Habakkuk wrote, "I will climb up to my watchtower and stand at my guardpost. There I will wait to see what the LORD says" (Habakkuk 2:1). In *I Told the Mountain to Move*, Patricia Raybon wrote, "God was there, standing behind the gate, inside the shadows, just out of sight, enormously quiet."

I know that if I am patient, I won't be disappointed. Yet I grow restless and impatient. I race ahead of God, unable to stand still long enough to see his face or hear his voice.

I've found that my impatience is one of the greatest obstacles in my relationship with God. Erwin McManus, an artist and postmodern futurist, wrote, "Often we miss the undeniable work of God because we give up too soon." I might hesitate and wait a few moments, but then I grow impatient and race off to something else. And usually I'm racing off to something trifling while missing what is truly significant.

How long are you willing to wait for the most important, powerful, life-changing connections in the universe? Five minutes? An hour? Twenty-four hours? Those who have learned to wait never regret it. Those who wait and absorb the stillness of the desert, allowing the supernatural to seep into their hearts, find that his presence is suddenly everywhere.

When I wait for God and let go of my all-important timetable, an amazing thing happens. I feel peace—a deep, embracing, merciful type of peace. Paul calls this a peace that "exceeds anything we can understand" (Philippians 4:7).

Life is like a storm, catching me in its grip and tossing me about. But if I move to its center, I can actually escape its wrath in the incredible stillness I find there. God is at the center of the storm.

I think we're a bit like the disciples as they took Jesus across the lake in their boat. Everything started out smoothly, but suddenly they found themselves in the midst of stormy weather. The wind was fierce and the waves were high. These guys were fishermen; they were used to rough water. Yet this situation stole their confidence and undermined their peace. Things seemed to be out of control. But Jesus simply said, "Be still!" and immediately there was a great calm (see Mark 4:35-41).

I love this story! Maybe it's because life seems so full of stormy weather. I want to have Jesus step up to me, put his hand on my shoulder, and say, "Be still!" I want to feel that great calm, even when the wind is howling and the waves are pushing my boat around.

So now when I feel the pressure of life weigh heavily on me, I focus with every ounce of my being on the reality that God is in control. I've learned to literally stop and take a deep breath. I push away all the expectations and responsibilities and activities that swirl around me. I remind myself that I don't need to race or worry. I don't even need to motivate or manipulate. I just need to sit back, find the eye of the storm, and let go. That's what trust is all about—just letting go.

The apostle Paul said, "Let the peace that comes from Christ rule in your hearts" (Colossians 3:15). By allowing myself to be still, my pulse slows, my eyes open, and my heart becomes more alive. And I have discovered, through good times and bad, that I can trust God more than I can trust anything or anybody else.

So I open myself to his stillness and let it work its way into my every thought and emotion. Sometimes I even feel a tingle in my gut as the stillness of the desert transports me beyond my everyday challenges and transforms me into a deeper, more meaningful person.

DAY 20

SILENCE

Silence is the discipline by which the inner fire of God is tended and kept alive.—HENRI NOUWEN

SILENCE CAN BE DEAFENING.

The most powerful thing I found when I was in the desert was the enormous silence. It surrounded and swallowed me. It made me nervous. Maybe this is because I'm shallow and addicted to noise and distraction. I'm afraid of silence, yet I long for it.

Noise stirs me up, draining and depleting my energy. It contaminates and corrupts much of what is holy. But escaping the noise allows me to breathe and relax. I desperately need times of silence—daily, weekly, and monthly. When life gets too loud, I often slip into my bedroom to journal or meditate. In the quiet, I can process and ponder. As soon as I shut the bedroom door, I'm aware that I'm shutting out all the distractions and distortions that keep me from connecting with God. I know I can connect with him anywhere, but it certainly happens more easily when things are quiet.

Other days I leave my house and hike deep into my backyard

to capture the silence. I stroll past the daylilies and cherry trees. Sometimes I sit on the footbridge, listening to the water rush below my dangling legs. There's calm in the sounds of nature, which are so different from the noises of civilization. This backyard silence is broken only by smooth, subtle sounds that don't demand my attention or force themselves upon me like city sounds do.

Silence is crucial to health. It provides the foundation of emotional, intellectual, and spiritual growth. As seventeenth-century French mathematician Blaise Pascal wrote, "The sole cause of man's unhappiness is that he does not know how to stay quietly in his room." And I would add this: his backyard, his desert, or anywhere he can ease into times of silence.

Without silence, the supernatural seems distant and unreal, even appearing to be simply an illusion. Yet when I'm wrapped in silence, I discover that all the trappings and trinkets of this world, not God, are the illusions. Silence ultimately leads me to God because when all is quiet, I'm best prepared to linger in God's presence, savoring the sweetness of the supernatural. I believe God loves these moments when just the two of us connect and communicate.

Silence opens my ears and makes room for listening. G. B. Duncan wrote, "God still comes where he can find someone quiet enough to listen and alone enough to heed." We need silence to hear that still, small voice that is so easily missed. The further I am from the noise of this world, the easier it is to hear. God is constantly speaking. He fills my silence with his words—elegant, profound, life-changing words.

In *The Intimate Journey*, Joel Warne wrote, "Hearing God requires patient, open-minded, and brave listening. It requires releasing safe agendas and stepping through sometimes scary doorways into a bracing new world that fills our lungs with heavenly air." So listen carefully to what God is saying. Be attentive and receptive to all that God is sending your way.

The night was silent, and I was fast asleep. Out of nowhere something woke me. I sat up and looked at the clock: 2 a.m. I put my head back on my pillow and closed my eyes.

Steve, call Dave!

It was a soft voice in the back of my head. I rolled over and tried to ignore it.

Steve, call Dave!

This time, the voice held a sense of urgency. Again I tried to ignore it as various thoughts raced through my mind: This is stupid. It's 2 a.m. I haven't talked to Dave in over a year. I can't call Dave unless I have a good reason. I'm just going back to sleep. Then, before I could close my eyes, the voice returned with an intensity that forced me to my feet.

Call Dave now!

Somehow I knew this was God's voice. I didn't want to obey, but I knew I had to. So I looked up Dave's number and called him.

Dave immediately answered, "What?"

"Hey, this is Steve," I said sheepishly. "I know this sounds weird, but something told me to call you."

"I'm glad you called," said Dave. "It hasn't been a good night."

"Why?" I asked.

"Well . . . I'm sitting here in my bedroom with a loaded pistol. Just before you called I decided to end it all. I told God that if he wanted me to live, he'd better do something quickly. I pulled back the hammer, put the gun to my head, and counted, 'One . . . two . . .' but just as I started to say three, the phone rang."

Dave and I talked for an hour. By the end of the conversation, he had pledged himself to a new start. He'd regained hope.

"Thanks for listening to God," he said just before we hung up.

When God speaks, we are foolish not to listen. We need to be like young Samuel, who heard God's voice and said, "Speak, your servant is listening" (1 Samuel 3:10). I believe God loves to speak into our lives. He is simply waiting for us to slow down and listen. As we settle into silence, God draws us beyond the emptiness of this life into a world where angels tiptoe and impossibilities thrive. His voice is mysterious and miraculous and magnificent. It's like none other.

In *Christian Perfection* François Fénelon wrote, "God does not cease speaking, but the noise of the creations without, and of our passions within, deafens us, and stops our hearing. . . . We must bend the ear, because it is a gentle and delicate voice, only heard by those who no longer hear anything else." The spiritual journey becomes meaningless if God is not speaking and leading.

God may use any of the five senses to get our attention. Yet I can be so easily distracted and dulled to his messages. They stand right in front of me, but I'm oblivious. Fortunately, he refuses to give up. Sometimes his disclosures are obvious and sometimes they're subtle; sometimes they're unusual and sometimes they are most ordinary. God speaks through creation, beauty, ideas, people, events, imagination, intuition, emotions, dreams, visions, Scripture, passion, prayer, conscience, conviction, coincidence, music, stillness, silence, or hardship. His means and methods are limitless. When he speaks, things happen. He forms, bends, breaks, or transforms our world and us.

Sometimes God speaks with such power that it stops me in my tracks, forcing me to listen whether I want to or not. But more often he speaks to me indirectly. Ben Campbell Johnson wrote that God's way of speaking to us may come "from ideas that appear in our minds, to events that occur in our lives, to hearing through others the voice of God." God can use anything that happens in our lives to communicate to us. He is constantly speaking in a million different ways.

The core issue is not whether his voice is real; the core issue is whether we are willing to pay attention and be open to his message. So let us listen . . .

Patiently: Know that God speaks when and how he wishes. He is not bound by our timetables. As a friend of mine says, "God is rarely early, but he's never late."

Expectantly: We can be confident that God will speak to us in one way or another. He is continually present; he is not distant. He is simply waiting for the perfect moment to break through to us.

Carefully: We must actively pay attention. The noise of this world is sometimes so loud that it drowns out God. We must also be careful not to confuse our desires with God's voice.

Excitedly: God has great things in store for us. He yearns to speak wisdom, joy, encouragement, and peace into our lives. He has amazing, wonderful things in store for us if we only listen.

If you are serious about risking faith, you must go to the desert. You must learn to absorb the silence and practice the art of listening. God wants to guide all of us toward good and direct us away from evil. He wants to teach, comfort, direct, warn, encourage, and enlighten. God wants to break through; he's simply waiting for us to be ready.

DAY 21

LIFE IN THE WILDERNESS

Saint Anthony wanted desperately to encounter God in a more authentic way. He was born about AD 251 to a prosperous Egyptian family. At the age of twenty, in an attempt to plunge deeper into his relationship with God, he left his home to wander alone in the desert and lead a solitary life. He believed that only in the desert could we "always have God before [our] eyes."

At the age of thirty-five, he went even deeper into the desert. Saint Anthony is frequently considered to be the father of Christian monasticism. Through his example and encouragement, a number of men and women left their towns and villages to seek God in the solitude of the desert. During the next two hundred years, groups of hermits scattered throughout the wilderness areas of Northern Africa and the Middle East. Known as the Desert Fathers, they dwelled in small, isolated communities and devoted themselves completely to God without distraction.

Here they bared their souls with ruthless honesty, wrestling to free themselves of the cares and comforts of this world. These early monks did not want an ordinary faith. They desired, with a single-minded passion, to see beyond the physical, natural realm. They yearned to touch God and to allow God to touch them. That's ultimately what the desert is all about.

In the same way, God waits for each of us in the desert. The desert is the borderline between heaven and earth. It is a place where God draws us close. We all need a desert—a place to be alone with God. It may be hard to find in our everyday world, but it has never been more necessary. Without a desert, we're destined to ordinary faith. But in the empty, desolate places of the desert, we are free to walk a different road and risk a real faith.

VERSE TO REMEMBER

I will fill the desert with pools of water. Rivers fed by springs will flow across the parched ground.

—ISAIAH 41:18

QUESTIONS TO PONDER

+ God, out of his great goodness, gives us the desert, but many of us struggle with entering into it. A wilderness seems too hard, too desolate, too frightening. Is God calling you there? What would your desert look like? What do you hope to learn there?

+ How might you practice solitude, stillness, and silence in your daily life?

+ In the desert, how might you gain:
  a realization of self?
  a compassion for others?
  a connection with God?

QUOTE TO INSPIRE

To be brought into the zone of the call of God is to be profoundly altered.—OSWALD CHAMBERS

05 | WELCOME HARDSHIP

"Times of adversity are always
times of opportunity."

—WARREN WIERSBE

DAY 22

TROUBLE HAPPENS

> Hope knows that if great trials are avoided, great deeds remain undone and the possibility of growth into greatness of soul is aborted.—BRENNAN MANNING

IT WAS JUST A SLIGHT EYE INFECTION.

Nothing to worry about, except the tiny infant was only six months old. The young parents wanted to be safe, so they took Fanny to the doctor. Unfortunately the doctor was poorly trained, and his remedy permanently blinded the baby. A few months later her father died, forcing her twenty-one-year-old mother to hire herself out as a maid.

Even as a teenager, Fanny Crosby wrote about how happy she was. She considered herself blessed to be blind. She became a teacher at a school for the blind, but her true passion was helping the poor. When people asked her about her handicap, she would often reply, "It was the best thing that ever happened to me."

Fanny's lack of eyesight gave her an inner strength and commitment to God. She once wrote, "If perfect earthly sight were offered me tomorrow I would not accept it. I might not have sung hymns to the praise of God if I had been distracted by the beautiful and interesting things about me."

During her lifetime, Fanny met with presidents, generals, and other dignitaries. She also wrote nearly nine thousand hymns, including "Blessed Assurance," "Safe in the Arms of Jesus," "To God Be the Glory," and "I Am Thine, O Lord." Her philosophy toward difficulty and adversity is reflected in lines such as, "God will take care of you . . . through sunshine and shade," and "Bring Him your burden and you shall be blest."

Fanny Crosby's greatest triumphs were the result of her greatest tragedy. I desperately want to live by the attitude she had, yet when hardship comes into my life, I am much more likely to be frustrated, angry, depressed, or overwhelmed. Feeling great about difficulties doesn't come naturally to me, and thanking God for them seems downright absurd.

Nearly two thousand years ago James wrote, "When troubles come your way, consider it an opportunity for great joy" (James 1:2). Joy? Like most people, I do everything I can to avoid adversity. Difficulties seem tragic and dreadful.

Too often, I'm a weak and wimpy Christian because I don't take advantage of hardships. I don't allow them to shape my journey into something supernatural, and I don't even try to understand what God might be doing.

Difficulties stretch us and deepen us and make us better people. George Meredith said, "There is nothing the body suffers the soul may not profit by." I think most of us realize that this is true, but we still pray that God will protect us from all the difficulties and dangers that might come our way.

No one wants a hard life. But maybe that's exactly what we need. Maybe that's what leads us forward. Maybe that's the heart of risking faith.

What if we began to view hardship as a friend rather than an enemy? What if a deeper life and an extraordinary faith only come when we welcome hardship? What if pain and suffering actually strengthen us and make us more authentic?

If this is true, we need not resist, resent, or fear difficulty. Instead, we can accept the fact that growth occurs more when we are challenged than when we are comfortable. The more we truly understand the purpose of problems, the more willing we will be to welcome them. Consider the following truths the Bible teaches about trouble:

1. This world is full of trouble (see Job 5:7).
2. We need not be fearful of trouble (see Deuteronomy 1:21).
3. Trouble will crush us only if we ultimately turn our backs on God (see Psalm 16:4).
4. Trouble is temporary (see 2 Corinthians 4:17).
5. God walks beside us through every trouble (see Psalms 9:9; 22:11).
6. Every trouble holds the potential for growth (see James 1:2-4).

There is a lesson in every trouble, and during difficult times I find that I'm much more open to these lessons. Pain makes us tender; it opens our hearts, our ears, and our minds. It frequently teaches lessons that can't be learned any other way. For as Benjamin Franklin observed, "The things which hurt, instruct."

Difficulties are inevitable—some are small and some are overwhelming; some happened long ago and some are happening right now. But trouble is not a punishment or a curse from God. It might be the consequence of my own mistakes, miscalculations, sins, or foolishness. Or it might simply be a reflection of the broken world we live in. Sometimes trouble is not my fault; it simply falls on me like rain—be it a sprinkle or a downpour. I can complain, grow angry, slip into depression, or grow cynical, but none of that will change the fact that life is full of . . .

+ accidents
+ losses
+ rejections
+ financial frustrations
+ job disappointments
+ abusive situations
+ personal failures
+ health problems
+ relationship conflicts
+ wounds and traumas

Each trouble is significant and painful. There is no question about it. Trouble rarely feels positive, especially when it first happens. One of the components of hardship is the unwanted emotions it brings with it: shock, anger, anxiety, depression, grief, guilt, hopelessness. How we deal with these troubles and emotions either takes us forward into new insights and experiences or traps us in the muck and mire of negativity.

Hardships may actually be God's greatest blessing to his children. Charles H. Spurgeon, a nineteenth-century preacher who experienced his fair share of physical and emotional struggles, wrote that many "owe the grandeur of their lives to their tremendous difficulties." In another place he wrote, "We shall never rise to the highest spiritual state by having all rain and no sunshine. . . . God puts the one over against the other, the dark day of cloud and tempest against the bright day of sunshine and calm; and when the two influences work together in the soul . . . they produce the greatest degree of fertility, and the best condition of the heart and life."

DAY 23

A REFINED CHARACTER

If there is any tenderness to my heart, it has come through its being broken.—JAMES EMERY WHITE

HARDSHIPS MAKE ME A BETTER MAN.

They improve who I am. I know this. It is through the difficulties of life that I have learned my most powerful lessons. Saint John of the Cross insightfully stated that "the benefits of the dark night will become evident, it cleanses and purifies the soul of these imperfections."

As I allow the dark night to cleanse and purify my soul, I'm also granted the following hard-earned qualities:

Patience: Adversity slows us down. It forces us to see the beauty and reality right in front of us. It forces us to wait— on time, on others, and on God. The apostle Paul wrote that difficulties are good because they teach patience (see Romans 5:3). They show that we are not in control and that all the anger and anxiety we muster only complicate the trouble. Patience comes when we face difficulties with the calm assurance that God is in control. Os Guinness, writer and social critic, encourages us to pray, "Father, I do not understand You, but I trust You." In patience we find peace.

Wisdom: Difficulties cause us to dig deeper for truth. They make us want to understand the hows and whys of life. John Patrick, an American playwright, wrote, "Pain makes man think." And as we think, we gain a perspective on life that raises us above a mundane, reactionary, misguided existence. Wounds give depth and wisdom, for more can be learned from adversity than most anything else. Pain etches its lessons deep in ways we cannot forget. If we embrace these lessons, we grow wise beyond our years.

Maturity: Prosperity creates spoiled, shallow, and sheltered recipients. But adversity, trouble, and hardship season the soul. They give us experience, and if we truly absorb the experience, we gain maturity. Hardship gives us perspective, and if we accept its lessons we become people of depth. Someone once wrote, "A smooth sea never made a skillful mariner." Rough waters teach us how to handle all other situations with a steady hand and a good attitude.

Courage: We develop courage by surviving difficult times and challenging adversity. As Mary Tyler Moore put it, "Pain nourishes courage. You can't be brave if you've only had wonderful things happen to you." Courage is the ability to face hardship without retreat. It does not complain or crumble. In fact, courage often gains strength through trouble. Our lives will either expand or recede based on how we deal with adversity. Courage is tested through difficulties, and faith grows strong when courage steps forward.

I know these qualities are admirable, but I tend to resist and resent the pain it takes to acquire them. Solomon wrote, "Fire tests the purity of silver and gold, but the LORD tests the heart" (Proverbs 17:3). God refines and even molds our character. Unfortunately the most effective means of making us better are heat and pressure. In a spiritual economy, character always takes precedence over comfort.

Life can be incredibly challenging and at times painful. Things don't always go our way. Sometimes they tear us apart. The issue isn't the adversity; it's our response to it. Every adversity is an opportunity to rise above the circumstances and demonstrate something positive. For as Abigail Adams, wife to the second president of the United States, wrote, "It is not in the still calm of life, or the repose of a pacific station, that great characters are formed. . . . Great necessities call out great virtues."

DAY 24

A DEEPER COMPASSION

You can only help others in proportion to what you
yourself have suffered.—WATCHMAN NEE

IT WAS A BEAUTIFUL SATURDAY MORNING.

The boys and I were going to build a retaining wall in our backyard, so we borrowed my friend Roy's truck and went to Home
Depot to pick up fifty concrete blocks. Each block was about forty
pounds, and just as we were almost finished loading them into the
back of the truck, something snapped. I heard a pop in my back,
my legs gave out, and I found myself crumpled on the ground with
the most excruciating pain shooting up and down my spine.

Fifteen-year-old Dylan rushed to my side and kept asking, with
a certain panic in his voice, "Are you okay, Dad? Are you okay?"

I wanted to answer and reassure him, but the pain was too
great to talk. I just lay there, gritting my teeth hard and hoping
I wouldn't pass out. Ten minutes later I could move enough that
Dylan helped me get behind the steering wheel of the truck. Focus-
ing with every ounce of attention I could muster, I drove the ten
minutes to our home. But then I couldn't move out of the truck;

in fact, I couldn't move at all. Tami and Dylan carried me to our van and drove me to the emergency room.

My back injury, though painful, was not serious. Within three weeks I had returned to normal, except for one factor: I now have a deeper compassion for those who suffer from severe or chronic physical pain. I used to have an *intellectual* empathy. My mind connected with their pain, but my identification was cold and distant. Now I have an *emotional* empathy, in which my heart actually feels their pain. It's no longer just their struggle; it's *our* struggle. Because we have shared the experience of pain, we are brought closer to one another.

When we have personally experienced the difficulties of life— fear, rejection, betrayal, shame, loneliness, hurt—we develop a gentle heart toward others in pain. Mitch Albom's best-selling book *Tuesdays with Morrie* chronicles the final months of seventy-eight-year-old Morrie Schwartz's life. As he lay dying of ALS, Morrie couldn't move his legs or feed himself or do most of the things we take for granted. Yet Morrie insisted on living each moment to its fullest and reaching out to others. In the midst of his struggle Morrie said, "Now that I'm suffering, I feel closer to people who suffer than I ever did before. . . . I feel their anguish as if it were my own."

Adversity will either harden or soften the heart. If we are hardened, we grow angry, depressed, and bitter. We become resentful and negative. We push others away—ignoring, criticizing, and neglecting their needs. As we are hard-hearted to others, we become hard-hearted to God. Jesus says that when we show compassion to those around us, it is the same as showing it to him (see Matthew 25:34-40).

If I want to get serious about my faith, I know I have to allow wounds and trouble to make me more compassionate toward others. Through personal adversity, I can gain patience, gentleness, and understanding I won't be able to gain any other way. When I see someone in a difficult situation, I know it could just as easily be me. And I recognize from my own experience how much they need comfort. As Paul wrote, God "comforts us in all our troubles so that we can comfort others. When they are troubled, we will be able to give them the same comfort God has given us" (2 Corinthians 1:4).

Because I have personally experienced difficult things in life, I'm better able to develop a gentle heart toward others in pain. I can see it in their eyes and hear it in their voices. It's hard to ignore their quiet cries for help, because I've been there and I remember my own pain. Suffering makes me sensitive to others who are hurting, and their pain becomes my pain. I want to help.

Compassion walks alongside others, trying to understand their hearts, reaching out and showing mercy. Compassion has empathy and sensitivity, and is willing to cry with those who weep. As Myla Kabat-Zinn has learned, "Each difficult moment has the potential to open my eyes and open my heart."

Personally I've learned that the more pain I've felt, the more I notice those in pain who have been around me all along. I also feel their pain in ways I never have before. I've found that I yearn to reach out to others by listening, helping, giving, encouraging, weeping—anything to let them know that they are not alone. I can no longer walk away unmoved.

When we reach out with compassion, we are to wrap ourselves up in "tenderhearted mercy, kindness, humility, gentleness, and patience" (Colossians 3:12). When I'm dealing with difficulty, I yearn for someone to show me these compassions, and therefore

I'm eager to share them with others as well. Trouble intensifies the value of these virtues and my understanding of the impact they can have in the lives of those who are struggling.

Because of the wounds and hardships in my own life, I find that my heart remains soft and broken by the wounds and hardships of those around me. As Philo of Alexandria, who lived during the time of Christ, reminded us, "Be kind, for everyone you meet is fighting a great battle."

DAY 25

A REMINDER OF HUMANITY

[Pain] purges us and makes us know ourselves.

—JULIAN OF NORWICH

WE ALL HAVE SITUATIONS WE CAN'T HANDLE ALONE.

Hardships remind me of that. They take the wind out of my sails of self-sufficiency and push me into a harbor of dependency. Adversity forces me to look honestly into a mirror and own the frail side of my humanity.

In the 2001 movie *Black Hawk Down*, a U.S. helicopter is shot down in the heart of Somalia's capital city, territory held by a crime lord and his army. American soldiers try to rescue those in the chopper, but the firefight is heavy. Guerrilla forces spray the soldiers with machine gun fire from every direction, and the battle is bloody. A cargo truck moves in and loads up with wounded American soldiers. The officer in charge commands one of his men to get into the truck and drive it back to the military base.

"But I'm shot, Colonel!" the soldier says.

The officer looks at the soldier and yells, "Everybody's shot! Get in and drive!"

We all have weaknesses and wounds; difficulty is the spotlight that exposes them. We might feel it any number of ways, each of which reminds us of our humanity:

Physically: With injury, accidents, health problems, financial setbacks, imprisonment, addiction, and loss.

Emotionally: With depression, disappointment, fear, anxiety, shame, grief, and sorrow.

Cognitively: With negative attitudes, poor choices, loss of confidence, confused or faulty thinking, and self-destructive points of view.

Socially: With rejection, abandonment, betrayal, controlling behavior, abuse, and loneliness.

Spiritually: With moral confusion, perceived distance from God, guilt, the judgment of others, lack of grace or mercy, loss of faith, and spiritual dryness.

Adversity is a means of letting us know that we need help from other people. For hardship to meet its purpose in my life, I must face my fears, swallow my pride, and seek help. I know I need the company, counsel, and comfort of others. I need someone to stand beside me. Yet far too often I wait for someone to come to me, and when they come, I either push them away or do not even recognize their offer.

In *The Intimate Journey*, Joel Warne wrote, "To those undergoing trials, angels will be sent. But we must allow our angels to appear. It seems strange, but it is possible, in suffering, to be so busy protecting ourselves, to be so in-tuned, so intent on our defenses, that no angel sent by God for our comfort can penetrate." These angels may come in many forms: friends, family, neighbors, acquaintances, teachers, strangers, grocery store clerks, pastors, counselors, or even actual heavenly beings. If you need help—and at certain points we all do—accept it.

God wants to help us. He is patiently waiting for us to accept his help, for us to ask or reach out or simply seek his will in the midst of our struggles. Yet he doesn't always intervene when and how we want him to. God's agenda isn't to solve our situation as quickly as possible but to teach us as much as we are capable of learning.

During a rigorous game of racquetball not too long ago, I tore the ligament in my right ankle. The pain was excruciating, and I had to be in a full leg cast for two months. During that time I couldn't place any weight on my leg. I couldn't walk or drive or do many of the things I love to do. I'm an active person, and this drove me crazy. I felt trapped because if I wanted to do something, I had to ask for help. I hated feeling so awkward and embarrassed and weak. Yet if I didn't get assistance from others, I was completely helpless. I had no choice but to admit my dependence.

I think God puts me in such situations to show me how much I need help, both from others and ultimately from him. When all is well, I'm not as aware of just how desperately I need God. Prosperity and lack of hardship are the enemies of faith, for they make me lazy, proud, and selfish. Yet when trouble and difficulty encircle me, I know beyond a shadow of a doubt that I need him.

Oswald Chambers wrote, "God comes in where my helplessness begins." Hardship forces me to look up, taking me to my faith. Pope John Paul II said, "Faith leads us beyond ourselves. It leads us directly to God."

I frequently wonder how people can handle difficulties without God. Life is tough and the answers are seldom easy. Helen Keller learned through being blind and deaf that "a simple childhood faith . . . solves all the problems that come to us." But having faith did not mean she had it all figured out. It simply meant that she trusted that God was in control. Chuck Colson, founder of Prison Fellowship, wrote, "I don't have to make sense of the agonies I bear or hear a clear answer. God is not a creature of my emotions or senses. . . . I can only cling to the certainly that he is and he has spoken."

DAY 26

A DRIVENNESS TO PRAYER

A wounded deer leaps highest. —EMILY DICKINSON

DIFFICULTY PUSHES ME STRAIGHT TO GOD.

It forces me to my knees, where I can only cry out to him. And this prayer provides hope when all feels hopeless. It is a bridge that spans the greatest adversity, connecting me with the source of all strength, courage, comfort, and peace. When David was surrounded by troubles he cried out, "Hear me as I pray, O LORD. Be merciful and answer me! My heart has heard you say, 'Come and talk with me.' And my heart responds, 'LORD, I am coming'" (Psalm 27:7-8).

Not only does prayer connect me with the infinite and the personal, it pulls me beyond my pain. And this dialogue brings intimacy and meaning that deepen faith. I am led to say with Mary Gardiner Brainard, "I would rather walk with God in the dark than go alone in the light."

The most powerful prayers come from people with their backs against the wall. Adversity strips away pretense and pride, calling for us to put ourselves in the hands of God. Martin Luther wrote, "Except under troubles, trials, and vexations, prayer cannot rightly be made." This seems to be sadly true, for when all is smooth my prayers lose their passion. Yet when things get rough, I pray with all my heart. Maybe the old saying is right when it insists that "need teaches prayer." Desperation improves our perspective *and* our prayers.

Panic pushes me to prayer—in part because I don't know what else to do. When I've exhausted all other avenues, I run desperately to God. When my son Dusty was about four years old, he drank a bottle of medication. It was probably a half hour later that Tami and I discovered what had happened. By then Dusty was acting strange—one moment hyperactive and the next lethargic. We called the doctor and he told us to bring Dusty *immediately* to the emergency room, where a medical team would be waiting for him. I picked up Dusty and ran for the car. As I set him in the passenger's seat, he passed out. I woke him up and took off toward the hospital, driving far above the speed limit. I didn't care about anything at that moment except making sure my son was okay. The windows were open, the radio was blaring, and I was shaking him to keep him awake.

"Dusty, stay awake," I yelled. "Focus on me. I love you. You can't fall asleep." Yet in spite of my panicked efforts, Dusty's eyes rolled back into his head and his body went limp. *Oh God, help me. Don't let Dusty die. Oh, please help him.*

Tears ran down my face. I yelled as loudly as I could for Dusty to wake up. I shook him. I threw bottled water onto his face. He opened one eye halfway, and my heart leaped for joy. I made the twenty-minute drive to the hospital in about twelve minutes. Once we arrived, nurses and doctors immediately surrounded him and went to work. I stood in the background watching them run tubes down Dusty's throat, give him shots, push on his chest, and take his pulse. I was afraid, and I prayed and prayed. At that point I knew I had no other option but to put this in God's hands and trust that whatever happened God would somehow see us through. Soon Tami was beside me, and we held each other close. Twenty minutes later the doctor said, "He's made it. The little guy is going to be okay."

As we cried out to God in our darkest hour, we discovered hope and peace and ultimately joy. We found that he hears our desperation and he answers our call, though not always in the way we want. When all seems hopeless, we are told in the book of Isaiah that God "gives power to the weak and strength to the powerless" (Isaiah 40:29). As I prayed for Dusty's life, I knew that God might not answer the way I wanted him to but he would walk through it with us, no matter what. I knew that I could trust him. Regardless of how he answered, I knew that I would not be alone and that I might even discover an indescribable joy in the middle of the pain.

Novelist Ted Dekker encourages us by saying, "Our faith makes the pain of this life inconsequential in light of the joy set before those who believe." And as Paul said, "Our hearts ache, but we always have joy" (2 Corinthians 6:10). For if we have hope, we can smile in the face of hardship. We realize that adversity is not a curse; it is a blessing. Believe it or not, hardship now becomes a part of the adventure—something to embrace and even to accept with joy. Troubles are now something we can actually thank God for. They deepen our faith, giving it meaning and credibility. Difficulty makes our faith real, because a faith that stays safe and avoids challenges ceases to be faith.

As we realize this, the words of Jean de la Bruyère take on an extraordinary excitement: "Out of difficulties grow miracles."

DAY 27

A STORY TO TELL

At those points where God has touched our lives, there seems to be a sustained spiritual energy that, when we revisit it, empowers us.—BEN CAMPBELL JOHNSON

My friend Jack hugs everybody.

He is always smiling and encouraging, but life has not been easy for him. Jack used to be a long-haul truck driver, and he loved the open road. When he was fifty-two, his right leg had to be amputated, and his company switched him to a desk job. Then the company downsized and eliminated his position.

No leg.

No job.

No money.

On top of this, Jack's mechanical leg didn't work quite right, so he would frequently lose his balance and fall flat on his face. "I'd lie on the ground and I'd be so angry," Jack remembers. "I'd wonder, *What's the use in getting up?*"

Soon Jack realized that if he kept fighting his adversity, he would become trapped in his anger and bitterness. So he accepted his difficulties and asked God to use them for something good. Now

Jack says that things in his life are even better than they were before his accident. God has taken his frustration and turned it into a wonderful opportunity. Jack now works as a chaplain for the elderly and the disabled. His struggle has cultivated in him a special gentleness and compassion, but it has also given him a powerful story. Without his hardship Jack would be still driving a truck. But today his story of triumph over tragedy is encouraging hundreds and hundreds of people.

Jack learned that a dark night can give way to a glorious sunrise. And a tragic wound can set the stage for a wonderful story. In a book entitled *Hope Rising*, Kim Meeder told a story of incredible grief when her father brutally murdered her mother and then took his own life. On the last page of the book she wrote, "Like standing on a mountainous trail, we can *choose* which way to go. . . . When confronted by pain, we can *choose* to take the descending trail that most often leads to a dark and lonely place. . . . Or we can select the ascending trail and, with some effort and perseverance, we can *choose* to allow our pain to motivate us toward becoming better people, to move us toward a better place."

When we choose the ascending trail, we transform our pain into a promise of hope. The best way to do this is by telling our stories. Stories should not be hidden away. Every story is important—a significant part of who we are. It can teach, encourage, and inspire others. It can change lives. When Jesus said, "No one lights a lamp and then puts it under a basket. Instead, a lamp is placed on a stand, where it gives light to everyone in the house" (Matthew 5:15), he was talking about our lives. Our whole lives. The good and bad, the successes and failures, the beautiful and ugly.

We should all be prepared to tell our stories at any time and in any place. I'm trying harder to do this. It's amazing how sharing my hurts can break down walls between people. It connects me with others and opens hearts. Pride and pretense have a tendency to disappear. Two sharers become wounded travelers, together seeking God's grace and comfort.

When my heart breaks over the pain of others, I desperately long to ease their pain somehow; my story links me to *their* story and pain. As I stand beside others, unwrapping my wounds, I believe I'm able to dispel a little of their isolation and loneliness. As Chuck Swindoll wrote in *For Those Who Hurt*, "With God's arm firmly around my shoulders, I have the strength and stability to place my arm around the shoulder of another."

As a psychologist, I listen to people's stories all day long. I love my job, and I love hearing these stories. They touch my heart and stretch my faith. I wish everybody could hear the stories of struggle and searching that I have heard. Stories have amazing power. But only if they are told.

Telling your story takes determination and humility. We must enthusiastically embrace our pain and share our story. It's easy to keep quiet and bury our pain deep in our hearts. Fear of rejection or embarrassment may reinforce our silence. But years of working with men and women in crisis have convinced me that wounds carefully hidden away end up hurting more. As we tell others what we have learned, others are given the opportunity to see that hardship need not destroy or sideline us. Instead it can make us and strengthen us.

There is excitement and freedom in embracing our wounds and turning them into something positive for both ourselves and others. Since we all have hurts and hurdles, pretending all is well seems ludicrous. My friend Tim has struggled with rejection and failure. Yet as he worked through it, he told me he *had* to tell others. He said, "It was really hard for me to come clean and talk about my hurt, but I wanted to help someone else out there."

It takes courage to stand up and speak out, but one person's sharing encourages others to do the same. It's the only way that the negative cycle of hopelessness, helplessness, and despair can be broken. It's the only way to discover the true value and importance of our own hardships. Such adversity should never be shunned or wasted.

DAY 28

BENEFITS AND BLESSINGS

If we had no winter, the spring would not be so pleasant.

—ANNE BRADSTREET

LIFE ISN'T ALWAYS FAIR.

At the age of thirty-two, John Bunyan was arrested for preaching at his own church and sent to the Bedford jail. The young man could have remained free if he had only agreed to stop preaching. Yet Bunyan insisted that he was doing nothing wrong, and as a result, he spent the next twelve years of his life in a cold, damp cell. During this time he refused to be defeated by his circumstances. He even wrote that God had turned his prison into a blessed place. Bunyan used his time in jail to encourage his fellow prisoners, pray, and write at least six books. He saw his adversity as a time to study the Bible and meditate on the spiritual aspects of life.

In 1672 he was finally set free, and there was a great celebration throughout the city. Yet three years later he was again arrested for preaching. All who attended his church were discouraged—all except John Bunyan, who saw this as just another opportunity to read, meditate, and write. During the next six months in the cold, dark, and depressing conditions of his cell, John Bunyan wrote his masterpiece and one of the best-selling books of all time: *The Pilgrim's Progress.*

Welcoming hardship is rooted in a deep trust that God truly cares. It is recognizing that a lesson is always hidden within the pain. It is searching for the benefits and blessings in the midst of adversity. It is accepting the fact that God never meant for this faith journey to be easy or risk free. He wants it to be amazing and stretching and enlightening and extraordinary and supernatural. He wants it to transform lives and bring people closer to him. But he never promises it will be easy.

This is part of what makes the journey so powerful. If it were an easy walk, we would not grow. But when the path is rough and steep and rigorous, the muscles of faith must stretch beyond the ordinary. They fight and flex, growing strong—so strong they can sense God's amazing, sustaining presence in the deepest pain and the darkest night. Those who are serious about an extraordinary faith will choose character over comfort, holiness over happiness, and sacrifice over security.

Sometimes I get so good at avoiding hardship that I fail to see its benefits at all. But George Müller, a nineteenth-century English evangelist and philanthropist, cut right to the chase when he wrote, "The only way to learn strong faith is to endure strong trials." I want a strong faith, so I know I have to embrace the challenge and stop looking for the easy way out. I have to actually go toward difficulty rather than away from it, believing that the benefits will far outweigh the pain.

I've got to be willing to face these hard times with strength and determination if I ever hope to build an extraordinary faith. I think I'm ready.

But then something cries out, *No I'm not!* I really want to be ready and willing to let God do whatever he wants to do, but this thought scares me. I want to be strong, and yet at the same time I want to run and hide.

Only when I focus on God's goodness can I relax and say, "God, give me your strength and perspective and peace. I can't do it alone."

Only then can I begin risking faith.

DAY 29

EMBRACING ADVERSITY

LIFE IS AN AMAZING ADVENTURE, full of excitement and discouragement, sweet dreams and wicked nightmares, smooth waters and turbulent storms. Of course I wish that all would be bright, that people would always be kind, and that challenges could be avoided completely. But this is not reality. Besides, it wouldn't be healthy.

Pain is a powerful teacher, and difficulties provide wonderful opportunities. I'm finally beginning to realize that a life without struggle may very well be a wasted life. It would be a life of selfishness and self-indulgence. It would be meaningless and quickly forgotten.

Yet my struggles force me beyond myself. They call me to reach up to God with one hand and out to people with the other. My struggles make my life complete. If all were smooth and easy, I might have no need to reach beyond my own skin. My struggles give life meaning and direction and beauty.

Ralph Waldo Emerson wrote, "When it's dark enough, men see stars." Are you ready to see stars? As you raise your head above your current circumstances, I pray not only that you will see a sky filled with stars, but also that you'll find truth, faith, and maybe even a few miracles.

VERSE TO REMEMBER

Consider it pure joy, my brothers, whenever you face trials of many kinds.—JAMES 1:2 (NIV)

QUESTIONS TO PONDER

+ Sometimes we work so hard at avoiding hardship that we miss the blessings God wants to give us. Looking back over your own life or the lives of those close to you, can you point to difficult circumstances that yielded amazing benefits?

+ Does your faith story include a good helping of struggle and adversity? How might you use your story to better connect with those around you? How have others used their stories to connect with you?

+ James Emery White says, "If there is any tenderness to my heart, it has come through its being broken." Have you allowed your heart to be broken? In what ways?

QUOTE TO INSPIRE

We do not for our part wish for health rather than sickness, for wealth rather than poverty, for honor rather than dishonor, for a long life rather than a short one; and so in all other things, desiring and choosing only those which most lead us to the end for which we were created.

—SAINT IGNATIUS LOYOLA

06 | PLUNGE DEEPLY

"Those who plumb the deep things of God discover true peace for the first time."

—CALVIN MILLER

DAY 30

DEEP WATER

> Deep is where we step out of the shallow tidepool of
> our hearts into the boundless ocean of God's power
> and presence. It is where we get beyond surface things
> and plunge into a deep relationship with our Creator.
>
> —HANK HANEGRAAFF

I LOVE WATER.

I think water is one of God's greatest creations. A tall glass of cold water quenches my deepest thirst. The pounding of a hot shower in the early morning wakes me up. The sound of water relaxes me. The sight of a blue mountain lake, a rushing stream, or a cascading waterfall excites me.

Some people tiptoe, carefully and cautiously, into shallow waters, slowly working themselves into it without ever getting fully soaked. As for me, I like to plunge into the depths. There is something soothing, refreshing, and cleansing about being surrounded by water. I love to swim in the Pacific Ocean in Mexico. Floating on the swells in the deep water is a wonderful experience, but getting past the waves can be a challenge. When the tide is coming in you can't just walk into the waves; they will slam against your body, shoving you back and maybe even throwing you to the shore. The key is to dive headfirst directly into the crashing waves. As you glide through the water, you'll soon find yourself beyond the force and floating in the calm.

When I think of God, I think of water. He quenches my thirst, wakes me up, relaxes me, and rejuvenates me. I can't live without him. Jesus wants his children to live full lives: "My purpose is to give them a rich and satisfying life" (John 10:10). Another time he says, "Anyone who is thirsty may come to me!" (John 7:37).

An ordinary faith sips from the cup and tiptoes at the edge of the water. An extraordinary faith plunges right into the deepest parts. Through hardship and enlightenment, the desert prepares us for the deeper things. Now the journey takes another turn and we move from the dryness of the desert to the depths of the ocean. Yet in such a journey we are never alone, for as Timothy Dwight, an eighteenth-century Congregational minister, reminds us, "The infinitely wise, great, and glorious benefactor of the universe has offered to take men by the hand [and] lead them through the journey of life."

The deep is constantly calling out. Thomas Kelly wrote, "For over the margins of life comes a whisper, a faint call, a premonition of richer living." I know in my heart that there must be more. Over time everything grows tired, dull, and old. Yet for some reason I still tend to only scratch the surface. It is not until I intentionally dive into the depths that I realize what life and faith are all about. And the deeper I plunge into God, the more dissatisfied I become with all that is shallow and superficial. This world suddenly appears so trite and trivial that I wonder how it could have amused me for so long. As I dive, I discover that the best aspects of the surface are only crude hints at the never-ending marvels and mysteries of the deep.

When we plumb the depths, we find authentic peace. And from this incredible, amazing peace come joy and satisfaction that open the door to a life that holds a hundred positive possibilities, such as:

Wonder: We can absorb and enjoy the miraculous.
Courage: We can step out and take risks.
Honesty: We can face our limitations and weaknesses.
Humility: We can give others priority over ourselves.
Patience: We can calmly wait for God's timing.
Compassion: We can accept and love anyone.
Contentment: We can relax and trust in God's provision.

Yet most important of all is the supernatural connection with our Creator that draws us deeper and deeper into him—his wisdom, his grace, his infinite secrets.

Eighteenth-century Quaker preacher John Woolman wrote, "It is good for thee to dwell deep." It may be good, but it certainly isn't easy. Even when I aim deep and do my best to get there, I find that I am fighting strong forces—fear, uncertainty, frustration, confusion, and distractions—that keep pulling me back to the surface.

One hot summer afternoon Tami and I were swimming in a remote natural pool high in the mountains of southwestern Oregon. We were having a great time, when suddenly my wedding ring slipped off my finger, falling slow-motion through the water some eighteen feet to the bottom, where it nestled between two large rocks. The water was crystal clear, and we could see the gold band gleaming where it landed. I dove down and swam toward it, but I couldn't get deep enough before being pulled back to the surface. I tried two or three times without reaching the bottom.

Then Tami gave it a try. On her first dive she went deep, grabbed the ring, and returned with a gleaming smile. Yes, she'd gotten it! The lesson was not lost: The deeper you go, the greater the treasure you find.

For those with determination and persistence, the rewards of plunging deep will be well worth the effort. Yet for most of us, depth is a process. I dove in three times and still could not touch the bottom, but each time I went a little deeper. If Tami hadn't gotten my ring, I'm pretty sure that sooner or later, with enough attempts, I would have gotten it. Likewise, plunging into God takes time. The longer you try with ruthless honesty and desperate humility, the deeper you'll go.

Those who have traveled ahead of us on this journey say that depth comes through constantly seeking him, knowing him, and embracing him. So as we stand ready to plunge deeply, let us join A. B. Simpson, who prayed, "Lord, lead us into the depths of Your life and save us from a shallow existence."

DAY 31

SEEKING GOD

The easiness and naturalness of trees and vines are shadows of His beauty and loveliness. The crystal rivers and murmuring streams are the footsteps of His favor, grace, and beauty. When we behold the light and brightness of the sun, the golden edges of an evening cloud, or the beauteous rainbow, we behold the adumbrations of His glory and goodness.

—JONATHAN EDWARDS

GOD LOVES TO BE FOUND.

When I was in grade school I believed that God mainly lived in churches, especially Baptist churches. I figured he sort of hung out there waiting for church services or having special meetings with the pastor. And of course his favorite place in church must be the sanctuary; after all, why would God hang around the basement or bathrooms? The big sanctuary, with high ceilings and stained-glass windows and an organ that could make those windows rattle, was surely a room fit for God.

Every Sunday morning I would sit in the pew beside my parents drawing cool pictures of spaceships and keeping an eye out in case God decided to make a special appearance. I was sure he'd show up sooner or later; he was just waiting for the perfect moment.

Most of the church services were kind of boring, except when the pastor told stories about famous Bible people. Suddenly things got exciting, but when the story was over everything got boring again. Sometimes between the stories, I'd search the sanctuary for hints of God. I knew he had to be there somewhere. At first the stained-glass windows seemed to be a good place to find him, especially when the sun hit them at the right angle. But our church didn't have fancy windows with pictures and words. It had simple panes of pink, white, and lavender—nothing very godlike.

Then I thought he might be behind the giant speakers for the pipe organ at the front of the room. Mr. Finn sat behind this old-fashioned organ on the left side of the church with his fingers flying over the keys and both feet pressing the pedals. He was amazing to watch. He looked grumpy most of the time, sort of like the wizard in *The Wizard of Oz*. But when he played the organ, he smiled and his eyes twinkled and his bald head glowed. When Mr. Finn was playing, the speakers made your heart tremble and your legs shake. I just knew God was ready to burst forward and do something. But when Mr. Finn had a heart attack and died, God left the speakers. Nobody could play like Mr. Finn.

Finally, on an unusually boring Sunday, I found God. He was in the spotlights embedded in the sanctuary ceiling. As I stared at them, I discovered that if I squinted just right, I could make rays of multicolored light spread across the whole ceiling. And if I tilted my head at a right angle, I could almost get the rays to touch the floor. These shafts of shining, gleaming light seemed so pure and powerful that I was afraid I'd bring the light right into people's eyes and blind them if I wasn't careful.

One Sunday morning, the pastor was reading from Genesis: "Then God said, 'Let there be light,' and there was light. And God saw that the light was good." With those words I knew I'd definitely found God. My dad saw me squinting and twisting my head. He poked me in the side and told me to stop goofing around. He said I was distracting people. I tried to tell him that I'd found God, but somehow I knew he wouldn't get it. So I decided to look at the light only when everybody was praying—that way I wouldn't distract anybody. I figured that maybe the secrets of the light should be kept between God and me. After all, sometimes adults just don't realize that God is hanging around waiting to be found.

A few years later I realized that God is much bigger than a church building. In fact, it is impossible to keep him contained in anything. God's presence is everywhere—in every face, every word, every circumstance, every blade of grass. Yet we are so used to living on the surface of life that we find it hard to see beyond the obvious to the subtle shadings that take us deeper. God has embedded some aspect of himself into everything.

C. S. Lewis said, "The world is crowded with Him. He walks everywhere incognito. And the incognito is not always easy to penetrate." Yet if every moment of every day we are determined to seek him, we can begin to see beyond our blurred vision and blindness. The prophet Amos wrote, "This is what the LORD says. . . . 'Seek me and live'" (Amos 5:4, NIV). Hosea, another prophet, challenged us to "plow up the hard ground of your hearts, for now is the time to seek the LORD" (Hosea 10:12).

Seeking God is the greatest of all adventures, surpassing all else I've experienced. It has opened my eyes to the realization that beneath every single thing there is . . .

a secret
a lesson

a beauty

a truth

Yet most important of all, everything provides a glimpse into God's magnificent character and his wondrous ways. Everything is an epiphany of something greater and deeper.

To seek God involves searching until we see him in all we see and hear him in all we hear. In this way we are constantly reminded of the closeness of his presence. He is always within reach. This makes searching both fun and fantastic. For as we seek him, we discover a hundred times a day that this is truly a supernatural universe and that God is just behind the ordinary. Yes, behind something as ordinary as spotlights embedded in a church ceiling.

DAY 32

FINDING GOD

> He is everywhere baiting, prodding us, luring us. He is
> playing hide-and-seek with heaven and earth, strewing
> clues all around, brushing the commonplace with the
> scent of Things Unseen.—MARK BUCHANAN

THERE MUST BE AT LEAST A HUNDRED WAYS TO FIND GOD.

There is no single formula that fits every unique individual. Different people seek God in different ways based on their strengths and passions and personalities. Some seek him through the simplicity and intricacies of nature . . . or through prayer and fasting . . . or through relationships and community . . . or through music and dance . . . or through rituals and traditions . . . or through reaching out to the poor and downcast . . . or through excitement and celebration . . . or through art and creativity . . . or through sweat and hard work . . . or through study and meditation . . . or through sacrifice and generosity . . . or through pilgrimages to hard and holy places . . . or through pain and suffering . . . or through stillness and silence . . . or through acts of kindness and compassion—this list could go on and on, but I think you get the point.

This journey we are on has no meaning unless it is a supernatural journey. At the core of this journey is the unshakable determination to find God. Yet sometimes I am so easily distracted. Comfort and convenience keep me at the surface, clinging to the safety of what I know. I say that I'm not satisfied with this world, but I continually fall under its spell. Feeling good tends to take priority over finding God. Yet feeling good is meaningless unless it is somehow anchored to finding God. There is no true satisfaction without him.

Life offers plenty of invitations to seek God. Annie Dillard wrote, "Dazzlingly or dimly, he shows an edge of himself to souls who seek him." An extraordinary faith is a steadfast journey to find God in every disguise in which he may camouflage himself.

Waiting to be found, God yearns for a personal, dynamic, exciting encounter with us. If we're willing to dive deep, he promises we will find him. But without such an encounter we are left trapped in the ordinary. Thomas Merton wrote, "For He is found when He is sought, and when He is no longer sought, He escapes us."

I hate it when I feel far from God. It scares me. Life seems less full, and each day is diminished and impoverished. And sometimes when I seek, I just can't seem to find him. There are times when I walk through a desert and it is alive—I hear his voice or feel his presence. But other times it seems dead—totally, absolutely, completely dead.

I can remember one particular desert in my life, a time when God seemed so distant that I wondered if he even existed. Before this time, God had opened doors and we walked through them together. I had cried out to him for wisdom, peace, joy, strength, and encouragement, and he had answered in ways over and above what I ever thought possible. During those times, his presence surrounded me, his voice directed me, and all seemed well. Then without warning, things around me started to fall apart. I stood in shock and disbelief. How could everything be so good one moment and so bad the next? It just didn't make sense.

So again I cried out to God. *What have I done wrong? What have I done to deserve this? Show me my failure so I can make it right.* I waited for God to come to me, but he did not come. I listened, but he was silent. I cried out again and my words seemed to bounce back off the heavens.

Where was God? Why wouldn't he reach out and touch me like he had in the past?

Maybe he wasn't listening or he didn't care anymore. Was he punishing me?

I felt abandoned and terribly alone. I wanted a sign, an encouraging word, a comforting touch—anything to let me know that I was not alone. But nothing happened. My heart ached, my head throbbed, my body felt weak. *What good is God if I can't find him?* A month passed, three months passed, six months passed. *Why would a loving, good God leave me alone for so long?*

Even though it felt fruitless, I kept pressing forward through the endless desert. Somewhere in my heart I think I knew that if I refused to give up and continued to dive deep, sooner or later God would show up. But I wasn't sure just how long I could keep up the struggle. It felt too hard and I felt too tired.

Nine months of emptiness passed, and I reached a point where I simply couldn't go on. One morning as I cried out once again in my desperate attempt to seek him, he was there. He simply slipped into my room and surrounded me with his presence. He didn't come with a spectacular burst of fireworks or a shout of triumph or a flash of brilliant insight. He was just there. And suddenly I felt as if everything was again as it should be. I smiled. I never knew why he left and what brought him back. Some tell me that he never left but that I had simply lost my focus. Maybe they are right.

Everything we experience is an opportunity to draw closer to him—even desert times. The more we seek him, the more we are aware that our every experience should draw us closer to him. The more we see his greatness and majesty, the more our hearts are stirred to seek him. In *Leap Over a Wall*, Eugene Peterson describes David's relationship with God: "Every event in his life was a confrontation with God." This is how it should be for all who plunge deeply: Every sight, every sound, every thought, and every event in our lives should be an encounter with God that draws us further from the surface and deeper into his presence. Yet to do this we must see life through new eyes, unclouded by the pageantry and presuppositions of this world. We must join the prayer of Saint Aelred of Rievaulx, a twelfth-century British monk, who cried out, "Lift the scales of ignorance from my eyes, that I may see you."

DAY 33

KNOWING GOD

The healthiest and most fulfilled pursuit of life is . . .
to connect with [God] as intimately as possible.

—JOSEPH STOWELL

"WHERE IS GOD?" I ASKED FIVE-YEAR-OLD DUSTY.

"Up in heaven," he answered quickly, pointing to the sky.

"Where else is he?"

"In my heart," he said as he pointed to his chest.

"How do you know he's in your heart?"

"I can feel him there," Dusty said with a confidence that indicated the issue was settled.

Children seem to know things that adults struggle to believe. Maybe this is why Jesus told his disciples to develop a childlike faith. Children trust; they don't have to figure out all the details or understand every situation.

As adults, we forget that we don't have to know everything to know something. Knowing God does not imply that we can ever define him (for he is beyond our definitions) or explain him (for he is beyond our explanations). To know God is to accept that he is beyond our ability to comprehend. We may know his presence, but we cannot grasp the complexity of his being and doing. In fact, I've actually found that the closer I move to God, the more I realize how little I really know. Yet to know just a speck of the infinite is to know a great deal.

Nobody knows everything about God. And anybody who claims to know even half that much is lying. Usually the people who claim to know the most actually know the least. Those arrogant, super-religious people who claim that God is on their side or that God supports their political agendas don't really know God. They only know a god whom they've made up and crammed into their own narrow mold. Their god is small and shallow and simplistic. This is not the type of god I want to know.

As I begin to plunge deeply, I find myself surrounded by thoughts and feelings and sensations of God. And I quickly discover just how overwhelming he is in every way. As I dive and drift, allowing myself to grow accustomed to him, I truly begin to know him.

Yet the challenge and frustration of this relationship is that when I speak about knowing God I must accept the fact that my attempts to know him will always be limited and partial. I can never fully know him, but that doesn't mean I shouldn't try to know as much of him as I possibly can.

If I want to know someone, I might start by gathering information about who he is and what he does. This is also a great way to begin with God. Facts and data are good. Reading and studying are good. Then I might ask others questions about him. *When have you felt closest to him? What's he like? How has he impacted you? Do you trust him?* I listen to their stories and experiences. If I hear enough, and if what I hear sounds authentic, I start to feel as if I'm getting to know him better.

This fact gathering moves me close, but if I really want to know him I have to spend time with him. Truly knowing God involves personal, intimate connections. I have to open myself up and be ready for him to draw near. Ultimately, knowing God involves a relationship with all the challenges and intricacies and satisfactions that any relationship holds.

The closer we get to him, the more we know him. And the more we know him, the closer we get. As Lynda Hunter Bjorklund wrote in *The Hungry Heart*, "Knowing God is a process, the greatest, most comprehensive journey we can ever make in this life." The more we know him with all we are—through our hearts, minds, souls, senses, and experiences—the healthier and more alive we become.

Knowing God allows me to let go and relax. It takes away the pressure I often feel to order my universe, because I know he already has it ordered. The nature of my relationship with God and the degree to which I know him define everything about me. It all comes down to relationship, for the more I know him the more I . . .

+ trust him
+ respect him
+ reach out to him
+ love him
+ lean on him
+ realize how empty I am without him

Because of this, Paul wrote, "[For my determined purpose is] that I may know Him [that I may progressively become more deeply and intimately acquainted with Him, perceiving and recognizing and understanding the wonders of His Person more strongly and more clearly]" (Philippians 3:10, AMP).

The process of knowing God is a never-ending adventure that

becomes more exciting and rewarding with each step we take. If this journey ever appears dull, predictable, or anything less than fully satisfying, then we have stepped off the pathway and gotten lost in the woods. The prophet Daniel wrote that "the people who know their God shall be strong, and carry out great exploits" (Daniel 11:32, NKJV).

Knowing God is being aware of him; he is everywhere and in everything. I can know him better by paying close attention to all things that are true or right, challenging or intriguing, beautiful or full of wonder. I see him daily in sunsets and seashores, in people and poetry. If I bask in the sun, I feel his warmth. If I listen to the morning, I hear his voice. Anywhere and anytime I take the effort to really look, he is there. He is at church and in the desert and at the soccer game. He is in the books I read and the music I hear and the stranger I meet on the street corner. Each encounter makes me more aware of some aspect of the infinite God. The universe and all it contains reflect the awesomeness of who he is, giving me even more reason to keep my heart and mind open every moment.

DAY 34

WALKING WITH GOD

> We are faith-explorers of a country without borders, one
> we discover little by little not to be a place but a person.
>
> —BRENNAN MANNING

I USED TO LISTEN TO TALK RADIO.

I'd turn it on as I crawled into bed each night and let it put me
to sleep, which it usually did within the first ten minutes. The
show I liked to listen to had a brilliant host who interviewed fascinating people with insightful questions. He let his guests express
their thoughts and perspectives with only minor interruptions (in
my opinion, most talk show hosts talk too much). Yet periodically
the host would have an evening without a guest and listeners were
invited to call in. These shows went smoothly until a Christian
called. He or she would usually want to talk about hell and homo-
sexuals and hatred. I wanted to crawl under a rock.

I don't know if these people were really Christians or not, but
that's what they called themselves. They sure knew how to rant
and rave. The host just let them go on until they hung themselves.
They were often the most arrogant, rude, judgmental, and poorly
informed people I'd ever heard. They were pathetic examples of
Jesus, and quite frankly they totally embarrassed me.

I realize that I may be the one who is now sounding arrogant, rude, judgmental, and maybe even poorly informed—for this I beg your forgiveness. These callers might have been wonderful individuals with the best intentions in the world, but at the time I desperately wanted to call the talk show to apologize for their attitude. I wanted to tell the host that not all Christians were like the one who'd just called. But I didn't. I guess I was afraid that somehow I might sound as foolish and insensitive as they did.

Several years earlier, my good friend Jerry and I had sat in a noisy pub, contemplating this very thing: the various approaches of those who claimed Christian spirituality as their own. We hypothesized that there were at least five approaches and, though they were all good, only those who pursued the fifth approach deserved to be called "Christians" in light of the original meaning of the term in the book of Acts. The approaches we defined were:

The Talkers: These people talk about God along with Christian philosophies, traditions, and activities.
The Goers: These people go to church, Bible studies, or assorted other faith-oriented events.
The Believers: These people believe in God and have committed themselves to following him.
The Doers: These people do good things that are generous, sacrificial, and genuinely loving.
The Walkers: These people try their best to live like Jesus and walk in his footsteps.

Jerry and I assumed that all five of these approaches would agree with the basic tenets of historical Christian orthodoxy. Yet the challenge for all of us is to truly be *Christian* at all levels.

The word *Christian* has to go deeper than simply hijacking the name and putting it on a bumper sticker or T-shirt. The word involves being a "little Christ," or at least someone who is very much like him. We use this word so flippantly and carelessly that for many it has lost its meaning or been associated with things that would make God blush. I want to be a Christian according to God's definition, but I have far to go if I truly hope to claim this title. In the meantime, I want to get to know him more and more. And the best way to do this is to walk with him every day.

To really know God, not just to know about him or know of him, we must become familiar with and open to him—every aspect of him. We must try to grasp as much of him as our significant limitations allow. We must desire—desperately and passionately—to learn more and more about him. Walking with him allows us this opportunity. It is only as we walk with him that life begins to make sense and we gain a clearer perspective of all that surrounds us.

God defines all things, and apart from knowing him and who he is, our best observations are but random stabs in the dark. Walking with him and knowing him are joined hand in hand. The more we walk with him, the more we come to know him.

To know God we must plunge deeper, with a determination to understand him better than ever before. To truly know him we must draw close to various parts of his character.

God's face: This involves being aware of his beauty and majesty, his simplicity and complexity. It is to see, and even feel, his presence in a smile, a sunset, or a rugged mountain. The psalmist said, "Make your face shine down upon us"

(Psalm 80:3). Let us daily see his countenance, be reminded of his grandeur, and bask in his radiance. Let us never forget that his presence is constantly before us.

God's mind: This begins by reaching out for his guidance and direction, considering his thoughts and plans as we try to align our minds to his. Isaiah wrote, "'My thoughts are nothing like your thoughts,' says the LORD. . . . 'For just as the heavens are higher than the earth, so my ways are higher than your ways and my thoughts higher than your thoughts'" (Isaiah 55:8-9). The more we know God's thoughts, the more they become ours.

God's heart: This involves letting God's incredible love and compassion embrace us, and allowing his grace and mercy to become part of our hearts. Samuel said, "The LORD has sought out a man after his own heart" (1 Samuel 13:14). Let us be people like this. The book of Psalms tells us that "his faithful love endures forever" and "he loves us with unfailing love" (Psalms 106:1; 117:2). To know his heart is to let our hearts become like his.

God's voice: This involves listening to his call, his commands, his comfort, and recognizing them above all the noise and clatter of this world. Moses heard it in a burning bush; Samuel heard it in the dark of the night; David heard it in the thunder; Elijah heard it in a gentle whisper. God's is a voice like none other.

God's hands: This involves knowing that his ways are always best and relaxing with the confidence that his hands are tender and strong—sometimes healing, sometimes harsh, but always good: so very, very good. His ways are trustworthy, and as we take his hand we can face anything. In the end we can join the psalmist who wrote, "Everything he does reveals his glory and majesty" (Psalm 111:3).

If we can grab hold of these five aspects of God, we will truly begin to know small fragments of his immensity. As we continue to walk with him and get to know him, we'll never lose our fascination and awe for God. The thrill of knowing him will never subside. The desire to know him better will motivate everything we do. As George MacDonald noted more than a hundred years ago, it is impossible to know God as he is and not desire him.

DAY 35

EMBRACING GOD

Those who embrace God are in for the ride of their life.

—DAVID SWARTZ

IT WAS A FROZEN CHRISTMAS SEASON.

The winds howled through the gorge and blasted the valley with temperatures far below the freezing point. Yet my three kids, all under ten years old at the time, insisted on going shopping. So we bundled them up and braved the cold. As we entered one of the stores, a beautiful, life-size ceramic Nativity scene sat right at the entrance. The kids stood and stared at how real baby Jesus looked as he lay in the manger of straw. Then we moved off to other areas of the store, looking at books and games and toys.

Suddenly I realized that six-year-old Dylan was missing. I started a methodical search of the store, but I couldn't locate him. As each minute passed I felt that growing sense of panic in the pit of my stomach that we parents get when our children might be in danger. My heart pounded, my pace quickened, and sweat collected on my forehead. *Oh God, help me find him. Keep him safe.*

Then I turned a corner, and there he was. Suddenly all was well with the world. Little Dylan was just standing there, rocking the ceramic baby Jesus in his arms.

"What are you doing?" I asked.

"Keeping Jesus warm," he said as he held the baby close. He pointed out that every time the door opened, cold air blew on the manger. As I led Dylan back to the Nativity scene and insisted he place Jesus back where he belonged, Dylan looked at me with a worried expression and said, "People shouldn't do this to Jesus."

I've thought about Dylan's words many times since that day, and I think he's right. We need to embrace God and hold him close. Not because we need to keep him warm, but because he needs to keep us warm. The more we walk with God, the closer we want to get until even the most reserved and introverted among us yearn to embrace him. To embrace God is to do all we can to be as close to him as possible. It is to yearn, crave, hunger, thirst, and dream for a connection with him.

Jim Cymbala wrote in *The Life God Blesses* that "inside the human heart is an undeniable, spiritual instinct to commune with its Creator." This communion provides such peace, such fulfillment, that our souls feel a touch of heaven. The more we embrace God, the more our souls are transformed. Soon that communion grows from a desire to an urgent need to an absolute necessity. To be apart from him is to be lost and empty and devoid of all joy. To be apart from him becomes both intolerable and unthinkable. Saint Augustine wrote, "Desire only God and your heart will be satisfied."

Closeness to God shapes, seasons, and strengthens us. It turns our souls from something as common and breakable as clay into something as precious and spectacular as gold. As we embrace him, he embraces us, and we are never the same. His presence changes everything, especially us. All we are is transformed . . .

+ our thoughts
+ our feelings
+ our choices
+ our priorities
+ our vision
+ our hearing

In *The Presence Based Church*, Terry Teykl wrote, "God's presence defies the limits of our vocabulary and dwarfs our most unbridled imaginations. . . . His presence penetrates and imprints everything it touches. Never to be the same. It is the greatest experience one can have." This is an experience that stretches us and expands us, filling us with impossible possibilities and incomprehensible realities.

The closer we get to God, the more obsessed and amazed we become with the supernatural. Everything pales and becomes dull in comparison to his eternal realities. No matter how hard it tries, the physical world just can't measure up to the spontaneous splendor of the spiritual realm. Just because we were born into this world, breathe its air, eat its food, and walk its ground doesn't mean our spirits can't peer beyond the visible and touch the intangible.

This is what I secretly long for. I know that when I reach out to God and cling to him, my spirit comes alive. It leaps and dances and shouts for joy. It feels all the excitement and enthusiasm I felt when I first fell in love with my wife. That's because this *is* love. Love of the highest, purest, and most satisfying kind. This is what real living is all about.

As we embrace God, we melt into his arms. We finally realize where we really belong and how we have longed so deeply to be held by him. We come to know that this world is not safe or stable. Yet being close to God gives us that safety and security we have been searching for. Regardless of what this broken world may bring, God is there to love and embrace us. As he embraces us, we are invited to embrace him and therefore feel his love.

I want to embrace God. I want to show him that I love him, but I get lazy and selfish and distracted. My love doesn't look very loving. It is so quiet and incomplete. I end up loving my car and my house, my wife and my children, my freedom and my television, and sometimes even my dinner more than God. How foolish! What a hypocrite I am. I love God. I really do. But I frequently don't act like it. What's wrong with me? He gives me the desires of my heart. He blesses me when I'm discouraged. He loves me even when I'm a pain. What an incredible God! How could I not love him? Sometimes I wonder if I even know how to love him.

To love God is to reach out and embrace him. It is to take the love he has for us and reflect it back to him. Jesus said, "'You must love the LORD your God with all your heart, all your soul, and all your mind.' This is the first and greatest commandment" (Matthew 22:37-38).

Loving God is an act of appreciation for who he is and what he does. My love of God drives me forward on this journey. As I come close to him, I realize that God is more than enough; he is my everything. To love him with all I am gives me, and all that I experience, glorious meaning. I suddenly feel alive with a passion that enthralls my heart, energizes my soul, and enlightens my mind. To plunge into the depths of his love allows me to take my eyes off myself and let them settle on the source of all love. As I love him, his love makes everything better and brighter.

I love him because he is the one most worthy of love, but also out of gratitude for the immensity of the undeserved love he showers upon me every day. C. S. Lewis wrote that "a man's spiritual health is exactly proportional to his love for God." I'm ready to get healthy.

DAY 36

LIVING IN THE DEPTHS

DEEP WATER USED TO SCARE ME.

Any water that was over my head seemed more than a little dangerous. I loved the local public pool, but I was never brave enough to leave the shallow end.

But when I was about nine, my uncle Walt decided it was time I learned to swim. He took me to a narrow canyon where a rushing creek flowed between massive rocks and formed three or four deep pools. Even though he promised me the water was only six or seven feet deep, I was still terrified.

"If I jump in, I'll sink to the bottom and drown," I explained, as if Uncle Walt didn't understand the most rudimentary laws of gravity.

"If you jump in, you'll swim," he said nonchalantly. "But if you do sink, I'll pull you out and save you."

After staring at the water for what seemed like hours, I finally just took the plunge, hitting the water with a splash and sinking down deep before popping up to the surface. I didn't die! In fact, in spite of my initial fear, swimming actually became one of my most favorite activities.

And once I learned to overcome my fears and plunge deep, I discovered a world of adventure and amazement. There was no stopping me—diving, snorkeling, surfing, skiing, kneeboarding. I loved it all. And today, some forty years later, swimming is still one of my favorite things to do. It relaxes my body and brings freedom to my soul.

This is also what plunging into God does for me, but in ways that are so much more powerful and meaningful and eternal.

Plunging into God brings us close to him. This closeness defines who we are and all we experience. We grow deep as we go deep and become more conscious of him in every aspect of our lives. Sure, there are fears and doubts and mysteries, but that's what faith is all about. As we learn to live in him we discover it's the only place that makes any sense to live.

After all, deep water is the best.

VERSE TO REMEMBER

In him we live and move and exist.—ACTS 17:28

QUESTIONS TO PONDER

+ When we plunge deeply into extraordinary faith, we discover a brand-new world. How might going deeper affect your faith in the following areas:

  a nourished soul

  a cherished heart

  an empowered spirit

  an expanded perspective

+ The reality of plunging deeply makes it clear that this world is not our real home. It is simply a layover where we await our final flight to someplace bigger and better. How does this understanding change the way you live today?

+ Are you still clinging to the shore or limiting yourself to the shallow end of the pool? What would it take for you to plunge deeply into the life of faith?

QUOTE TO INSPIRE

Without a life of the spirit, our whole existence becomes unsubstantial and illusory. The life of the spirit, by integrating us in the real order established by God, puts us in the fullest possible contact with reality—not as we imagine it, but as it really is.—THOMAS MERTON

07 | GIVE BACK

"Love mercy; treat your
enemies well; succor
the afflicted; treat every
woman as if she were
your sister; care for the
little children; and be
tender with the old
and helpless."
—THEODORE ROOSEVELT

DAY 37

ACCEPTANCE

Humans are indeed an odd, entertaining breed of mishaps and blunders. . . . Yet as bizarre and screwed up as we are, beauty is threaded through our stories. Glory, dignity and grace bubble up from our souls.—STEVEN JAMES

"JUDY STOLE MY TEETH," ARNIE SAID IN DESPERATION, "and she won't give them back."

Arnie is a big guy. He used to be a boxer in the Army some fifty years ago, and he still looks the part. His face is marred with scars, pockmarks, and wrinkles. Arnie looks tough and sounds tough, but he has a heart of gold.

"Dr. Steve, why'd she do this to me? I've got to have my teeth. I'll hunt her down if I have to. It's just not right for a woman to run off with a man's teeth. It's just not right."

"One way or another we'll get your teeth back," I reassured Arnie.

"Oh, thank you, Dr. Steve," Arnie said. "I know that there are two people who can help me when I'm down and out: the Lord Jesus Christ and Dr. Steve. Well, I've been praying to the good Lord and he's not answering. So I knew it was up to you, Dr. Steve."

Arnie's pretty rough around the edges. He's been struggling with alcoholism since he was thirteen, and he yells a lot, especially when he drinks too much. Sometimes he does well, and sometimes he doesn't. When Arnie drinks, he does stupid things: He gets into fights with the police or crashes his car into telephone poles or visits strip clubs. One night he even ran naked through the streets yelling at the top of his voice, "The Russians are coming! The Russians are coming!"

When he does these things, Arnie usually ends up in jail or the psych ward of some hospital. And then he tells them to call Dr. Steve: "He's my friend. He'll help me."

Most people avoid Arnie—except the street kids he makes lunches for, the prostitutes he bails out of jail, and his fellow alcoholics he meets at the downtown AA meetings. I think it's sad that people don't get to know Arnie. They don't know that his father died when he was ten and his mother abandoned him when he was twelve. They don't know that he worked for the city of Portland for thirty years and never missed a day on the job. There's so much they don't know about Arnie.

People call him a drunk and a bum, an idiot and a psycho. But let me tell you, Arnie is a good man. He'd be the first to tell you that he has made a lot of mistakes in his life and he's as far from perfect as they come. But Arnie was made in the image of God.

People have argued for thousands of years about what being made in the image of God really means. Is it the ability to choose or create or care? Is it the desire to reach beyond ourselves or search the stars or stretch our souls toward the divine? I can't tell you exactly what it is, but I know it means something very special.

I think part of it is that God sees us as valuable and worthwhile, even if the people around us ignore us, mistreat us, or misjudge us.

People can be cruel, but God is love. Psalm 136 repeats twenty-six times that "his faithful love endures forever."

In first grade I won a gold star and a candy bar for memorizing John 3:16 out of the King James Version of the Bible: "For God so loved the world, that he gave his only begotten Son, that whosoever believeth in him should not perish, but have everlasting life." This verse was quite a mouthful for a hyperactive six-year-old, but I'd have done almost anything for a 3 Musketeers bar. As I recited the words, I barely understood what I was saying. Yet it struck me as amazing that God would love the whole world—even the people in Africa and India, even the old man who lived in the haunted house at the end of the street.

How does God do that?

He does it in part by seeing deeper and broader and clearer than any of us ever could. He has sharper eyes that are neither as clouded nor as distracted as ours. The first book of Samuel says, "The LORD doesn't see things the way you see them. People judge by outward appearance, but the LORD looks at the heart" (1 Samuel 16:7).

Yes, most of us are drawn to outward appearance. The heart seems too difficult and maybe even impossible for us to discern. So we take a shortcut and thereby frequently miss the grandest and most amazing of sights. King David asked, "What are people that you should think about them, mere mortals that you should care for them? Yet you made them only a little lower than God and crowned them with glory and honor" (Psalm 8:4-5).

I met Brian when we were in fourth grade.

He was a good kid who lived three streets up the hill from us.

Brian was shy and always hung out on the fringes. When all the neighborhood kids got together to ride bikes, play hide-and-seek in the woods, or go swimming at the community pool, Brian wasn't there. He just wasn't comfortable with crowds.

Brian didn't have many friends. In fact, I might have been his only friend. A few months after we met, he started going to church with my family. David, Brian, and I sat in the back row during the church service and drew pictures of space aliens and vampires. We were known as "the Three Musketeers" because the three of us were always together. On other days Brian and I threw darts, built forts in his backyard, hiked to the top of Mount Scott (which is really more of a tall hill than a mountain), or went to the movies whenever we could get his big brother to take us. Life was good, and we were as carefree and innocent as any two kids could be.

One fall we converted an old, abandoned chicken coop into a haunted house, and during the week before Halloween we charged people ten cents each to go through it. Brian and I were monsters with ketchup all over our faces to look like blood. My little brother said it was so scary that he almost wet his pants.

When we were in sixth grade, Brian's dad died suddenly. I think it was a stroke or a heart attack. His dad was a lot older than the other dads in the neighborhood, but none of us expected him to die. It was the first funeral I'd ever been to, and the body in the casket sent chills up my spine. But I wouldn't have missed it for anything, because I wanted to be there for my friend; I knew it had to be the worst day of his life. I sat beside Brian after the funeral and we both cried. We were buddies and I shared his pain. After all, isn't that what friendship is all about?

The next year all the seventh graders started at a new school. Everything was different—the classes were harder, the teachers were meaner, and the kids all tried to be cooler. Suddenly I had to look a certain way and listen to the right music and hang out with the popular kids. Anyone who did any of this wrong was labeled a loser. I hated junior high, but I had no choice but to play the game.

This is when I learned that Brian was a "retard." The first time I heard it I didn't take it seriously—everybody called each other names; it was just a part of the torture preteens inflict on each other. The kids started by calling him names behind his back, but soon they grew bolder and yelled "retard" at him as he walked down the halls. At first this made me mad. I couldn't believe how unfair and rude and harsh people could be. At first I defended Brian. But that was before I knew the rules.

As an "in-betweener," I wasn't cool enough to be in the popular group and I wasn't freaky enough to be in the loser group. The problem with being an in-betweener was that one misstep could send you sliding downward into the loser category, and once there, it was nearly impossible to claw your way out. So rather than risk my precarious in-between position, I learned to keep my mouth shut.

I had always known that Brian was a little slower than the rest of my friends. I knew he'd been held back in second or third grade, but I never thought anything of it. Brian was unique. He laughed long and loud. He'd burst into some old song and sing a chorus or two for no reason except that he loved to sing. He also wore clothes that didn't seem to match or fit right. He wasn't very coordinated, and sometimes he tripped and fell on his face. But Brian was Brian. None of these things had ever bothered me until now.

By Christmas I had completely caved to the peer pressure. When Brian called my house, I didn't return his calls. When he wanted to hang out, I told him I was too busy. When he said hi in the halls, I

ignored him. My family still took him to church for another year
or so, but nothing else was the same. I felt terrible, but I was afraid
that if I stayed friends with Brian everybody would think I was a
loser. What made me feel even worse was that Brian just accepted
my rejection without anger or complaint.

For the rest of junior high and high school, I just pretended I
didn't know Brian. After we graduated, I would run into his mother
periodically and ask her how Brian was doing. She always said
something like, "He's struggling" or "He's depressed" or "He can't
quite find his way in life." Then she'd say, "You ought to call him.
He'd really like that." But I never called him. Maybe I was embarrassed at how badly I'd treated him. Maybe I just didn't know what
to say. In the back of my mind I thought, *One of these days I'll call
him. I'll apologize for being such a rotten friend. And Brian will laugh
long and hard. Then we'll reminisce about the old days when we were
carefree and innocent.*

About ten years ago my mother called me on a hot July afternoon, shortly after Tami and I had returned from vacation.

"Steve," she said, "did you hear about Brian?"

"No," I said, suddenly concerned.

"He died last week."

"What happened?"

"An overdose of something. They think it might have been
suicide."

"Oh, no!" I said as my heart sank. "When is the funeral?"

"It was last Saturday."

"Oh, I wish I'd been in town."

Over the past few years I've thought a lot about my lack of love
toward and acceptance of Brian. The whole situation disappoints
and saddens me to this day. Sometimes it just makes me feel sick.

How could I have treated Brian that way? How could any human being treat another like that?

Acceptance is easy when it's comfortable, but sometimes it costs us something. In fact, love *should* cost us something—time, effort, money, convenience, and maybe even popularity. Compassionate acceptance is selfless and sacrificial. It focuses more on another than us. It cares. It reaches out.

I want to be a much more accepting person. But as long as I am concerned with what it might cost me, I will fail. My self-absorption and selfishness will stifle me, turning me inward. The apostle Paul wrote that we're to "share each other's burdens" (Galatians 6:2). This won't always be easy.

Jesus would have walked the halls of my junior high right next to Brian. If my faith cannot weather the hard things and show acceptance during difficult times, it is a pretty flimsy faith.

We may each be broken and battered, but we are also made in the image of God—all of us, every single one of us. Even Brian.

Even Arnie.

"Dr. Steve, do ya like me?"

"There's no question about it, Arnie. I definitely do!"

A big crooked smile beams across Arnie's face. "I think you're telling me the truth. And I want to thank you."

I give Arnie a hug. He wraps an arm around me and slaps me hard on the back. "I appreciate that, Dr. Steve," he mumbles. "I really do appreciate that."

"Arnie, I want you to remember that God loves you and the Bible says that nothing can keep you from his love."

"Not even when I'm falling down drunk?"

"Not even then," I reassured him.

"Not even when I do porn all night?"

"Not even then."

"But Dr. Steve, I've done some awful things. They've even kicked me out of the church."

"I know, but God's very patient. He doesn't care what the church does. He's a lot more patient than most church people. He sees your heart and he knows your struggles. He's not going to give up on you unless you give up on him."

"Dr. Steve, do you think God can do anything with a guy like me?"

"He already is," I tell him. "God has great dreams for you."

Arnie looks at the ground and chews the inside of his cheek. "That's something pretty serious to think about."

Oh, by the way, Arnie got his teeth back.

DAY 38

COMPASSION

Compassion is the strength and soul of a religion.

—KATHLEEN NORRIS

CHAD WAS THE KING OF THE NEIGHBORHOOD.

When I was thirteen, he was the oldest kid on the street and he was in the circus. We all thought this was the coolest thing in the universe. At the time Clackamas High School had a youth circus, and Chad was one of the star performers. He was a clown, a trapeze artist, a stilt walker, a juggler, and a unicycle rider. Chad would ride his unicycle up and down the street while juggling five or six bowling pins. He was amazing.

Half of our neighborhood was Catholic and half was Protestant. All the kids had a standing argument about who was better, the Pope or Billy Graham. Mike Hackett insisted it was the Pope because he had more money and owned his own country, but Sarah Schouten placed her vote for Billy Graham because he was on TV all the time and could play golf.

We argued about these things for hours—everybody except Chad. He said that religion confused him. His mother was Catholic and his father was Protestant, so he got baptized in both churches just to cover the bases. If you asked him about it, he'd say he wasn't sure what he was.

The Thompsons lived on the next street over from the rest of us. We called it the rich street. They had the largest house in the neighborhood, with tall ceilings, marble floors, and a beautiful grand piano in their living room. They went to a big Protestant church in downtown Portland, but they got in a big fight with the pastor about something so they left the church. They visited a lot of churches over the next six months and couldn't find anything they liked, so they decided to start a church in their own living room. They got a whole bunch of folding chairs and set them up in neat rows facing the grand piano. Then they invited everybody in the neighborhood to join them at 9:30 on Sunday morning. Since Chad didn't go to church anywhere, he decided to check it out.

Chad's alarm clock went off at nine o'clock. He quickly ate two bowls of Cocoa Puffs, grabbed the big black Bible his dad had given him for his fifteenth birthday, and walked over to the Thompsons' house. Mr. Thompson met him at the door wearing a black suit with a white dress shirt. He looked at Chad disapprovingly, staring at his wrinkled gray tank top, his well-worn Levi's, and his leather sandals. Then Mr. Thompson cleared his throat and said, "Chad, you don't look dressed for church."

Chad looked Mr. Thompson square in the eye and said, "I didn't know God had a dress code."

I'm sure Mr. Thompson didn't like that at all. "Why don't you go home and put on something more respectful?" he asked, slamming the door before Chad could respond.

When Chad told me what had happened, I was really angry. How dare Mr. Thompson slam the door on my friend? How dare he blame his rude rigidity on God? Jesus never would have treated anybody like that.

Chad went home and he didn't step foot in another church for more than twenty years. I tried to talk to him about God many times after that, but he wouldn't listen. He'd just give me a dirty look and say something like, "Mr. Thompson doesn't think I'm good enough for God; maybe he's right."

It's sad how much damage people like Mr. Thompson can do without even knowing it. Everybody knew Mr. Thompson was a Christian—at least that's what he told people. He talked constantly about God and church and the Bible. But he always looked stern and serious. Whenever I was around him I expected to get in trouble for something. Over the years I learned to do all I could to avoid him, and when I did see him I kept my mouth shut. Mr. Thompson reminded me that Christians come in a lot of different varieties and that I certainly didn't want to be the type of Christian he was.

The crux of Christian spirituality is compassion. Jesus said, "You must be compassionate" (Luke 6:36) and "Love your neighbor as yourself" (Matthew 22:39). He reached out to the lepers and prostitutes, the poor and handicapped, the rejects and outsiders. Those of us who are serious about following his example should do the same.

Compassion is crucial. And love is the lifeblood of our faith. As the 1960s counterculture anthem declared, "They will know we are Christians by our love." In this extraordinary type of faith . . .

+ people are more important than appearance
+ relationships are more important than rules

+ generosity is more important than accumulation
+ love is more important than being right

Philosophically I agree with these principles, but at times they are hard for me to swallow. Sometimes appearance, rules, accumulations, and just being right seem incredibly important to me.

In this selfish, crazy, narcissistic world, my greatest passion should be compassion. Jesus' words leave no room for ambiguity: "It is more blessed to give than to receive" (Acts 20:35). I want to be the type of person who daily gives kindness, encouragement, love, hope, and compassion. Albert Schweitzer wrote, "The purpose of human life is to serve, and to show compassion and the will to help others." He took this so seriously that at the age of thirty he decided to become a medical doctor and specialize in tropical diseases. He devoted the rest of his life to serving people in Africa. When asked about taking such a drastic step, he said he was tired of talking about love and wanted to actually put it into practice. At the age of thirty-eight he converted a chicken coop into an office, which grew into a hospital where he treated hundreds of patients with leprosy and sleeping sickness. Dr. Schweitzer gave much of his time and money to this center of compassion, which he continued to oversee until his death fifty-two years later. He wanted to live his faith with an authenticity that made his compassion obvious to all. And that is exactly what he did.

Mr. Thompson talked a good story, but Dr. Schweitzer lived it. Truth without love is empty and cruel; just ask Chad. Francis Schaeffer, a twentieth-century historian and theologian, said, "Biblical orthodoxy without compassion is surely the ugliest thing in the world." The last two thousand years have been packed full of cruel and hateful things done in the name of Christianity.

We should be ashamed for not being known throughout the world for our incredible love and sacrifice. I can be ticked off at the way Mr. Thompson treated Chad, but I've had my own moments when I've done no better. I tend to be kind when it's easy and convenient, but what about the rest of the time?

DAY 39

OUTREACH

> Miss no single opportunity of making some small
> sacrifice, here by a smiling look, there by a kindly word;
> always doing the tiniest things right, and doing it all
> for love.—SAINT THÉRÈSE OF LISIEUX

BRITTANY WAS FOURTEEN.

We were on a father-daughter humanitarian trip with North-west Medical Teams to Oaxaca, Mexico. We poured concrete floors in ten huts built on an abandoned garbage dump. We both found it to be amazingly sad, yet gratifying. At one hut, the mother walked several miles down the road and spent all the money she had to buy each of us a warm bottle of Coca-Cola. At another hut, a family mourned the loss of their father, who had hung himself the night before. At hut after hut, the families wept and celebrated and thanked us profusely when they saw their new floor.

When we finished our work, we handed out school supplies, hygiene kits, toys, clothing, and cookies to the children. One of my fondest memories is of watching Brittany, surrounded by nearly a hundred children, handing out our gifts. A huge smile covered her face as the children jumped up and down, trying to get her attention.

Each evening we would sit at an open-air café with the rest of our team, playing cards and telling stories until late into the night. This is where we met the street vendors, most of whom were children between the ages of four and twelve. They were a bit ragged but very polite and persistent. These kids would stand at our tables with their handmade friendship bracelets, hair clips, and other wares, begging us to buy "just one thing." As we visited with them they told us all about life on the streets in Oaxaca. After a few days in town, we fell in love with these kids.

As we neared the end of our time in Mexico, we celebrated Valentine's Day. We made reservations at a nice Italian restaurant and invited about ten of the children to join us. They were so excited. As we entered the restaurant, the waiters and waitresses looked at us in disgust as if to say, "Why would you bring these kids in here?" The headwaiter approached me and asked about the children. I explained that they were our guests, and he led us to an area at the back of the restaurant. We ordered seven gourmet pizzas and the children went to the bathrooms to wash up. After about ten minutes, we had to retrieve them because they had all gathered around the toilets to watch the swirling water. (Apparently they had never seen a flush toilet before.) Back at the table the kids placed the ice from the water glasses in their pockets and poured Tabasco sauce on their pizza until we could barely see the cheese. They laughed in delight and disbelief. The older kids taught the younger ones how to use the silverware. The younger children studied the room, with its white tablecloths and elegant wallpaper, in wide-eyed amazement. They devoured the pizzas, so we ordered more. As the meal was wrapping up, each child thanked us and hugged us. A number of them told us it had been one of their greatest days ever. I smiled at Brittany thinking, *This has got to be one of my greatest days ever too.* Brittany smiled back.

As we were leaving the restaurant, the headwaiter stopped me. "Thank you for bringing the street kids here for Valentine's Day. What you did was more important to those kids than you will ever know." Then he shook my hand. Not just a casual, perfunctory greeting, but a handshake full of meaning and appreciation. My eyes misted—not because what we'd done was so great, but because it was so easy. All it had cost me was the price of ten pizzas, a few hours of my time, and a willingness to reach out. Our ministry team agreed that it was one of the best investments we'd ever made.

Love notices needs. Love reaches out. Love is proactive. The challenge for all of us is to do ordinary, everyday things with care, compassion, and an outward focus. First, we must notice that every day we are surrounded by opportunities to say or do something kind. There is always a man by the side of the road, a woman with tears in her eyes, a person who is stuck or overwhelmed or in need of encouragement. Too often I am so focused on doing what I am doing that I don't even notice.

Second, we must be willing to be inconvenienced. Love takes time. It interrupts our activities and might even throw off our schedules. Dietrich Bonhoeffer, a German minister who was executed for standing against Hitler, wrote in *Life Together*, "We must be ready to allow ourselves to be interrupted by God. God will be constantly crossing our paths and canceling our plans by sending us people with claims and petitions." The question is whether or not we are willing to respond to his interruptions. The reality is that love responds.

When we can't or won't respond to the needs of others, we are in a dangerous spiritual state. Saint John of the Cross wrote that "at the evening of life we shall be judged by our loving."

An extraordinary faith loves the way God loves—in both ordinary and extraordinary ways. Loving certain people—family, friends, neighbors—may come easily, even if we are not consistent with it. But God's love goes beyond the obvious. Christian spirituality cares about people, *all* people:

1. **The poor:** "Oh, the joys of those who are kind to the poor!" (Psalm 41:1). "All they asked was that we should continue to remember the poor" (Galatians 2:10, NIV).

2. **The needy:** "The LORD hears the needy" (Psalm 69:33, NIV). "Be openhanded toward your brothers and toward the poor and needy in your land" (Deuteronomy 15:11, NIV).

3. **The weak:** "Help the weak" (1 Thessalonians 5:14, NIV). "Defend the cause of the weak. . . . Rescue the weak and needy" (Psalm 82:3-4, NIV).

4. **The widows and orphans:** "He defends the cause of the fatherless and the widow" (Deuteronomy 10:18, NIV). "Pure and genuine religion in the sight of God the Father means caring for orphans and widows in their distress" (James 1:27).

5. **The children:** "Let the children come to me. Don't stop them!" (Matthew 19:14). "He took the children in his arms and placed his hands on their heads and blessed them" (Mark 10:16).

6. **The foreigners:** "He shows love to the foreigners living among you and gives them food and clothing"

(Deuteronomy 10:18). "Show mercy and kindness to one another. Do not oppress widows, orphans, foreigners, and the poor" (Zechariah 7:9-10).

This should be just the beginning of our love and compassion. Mother Teresa of Calcutta said, "Let us touch the dying, the poor, the lonely, and the unwanted according to the graces we have received and let us not be ashamed or slow to do the humble work." This is what Christ would have done. This is what Christians should do. Whether you do it in Oaxaca, in Calcutta, or in your own backyard.

DAY 40

GIFT GIVING

LATELY I'VE BEEN MAKING AN EFFORT to befriend people who don't fit neatly into my comfort zone. I have come to truly love these people, not just tolerate them. It seems that the further I go on this journey toward extraordinary faith, the more I just need to give back. Loving involves embracing someone, fully accepting that person into your circle.

I might not agree with everything you might do or think, but I can still reach out to you, love you, and show compassion toward you. The challenge for me is to see the face of God in every person I meet.

Giving back to others might be one of the most important things we do in this life. It is putting faith into practice. It is trying to be like Jesus. Paul wrote that "love is kind" (1 Corinthians 13:4, NIV). So as I walk through each day I am committed to following the approach of James M. Barrie, who is best known for writing *Peter Pan*: "Always be a little kinder than necessary."

Therefore, to help me reach out more often, I have tried to implement the following seven commitments:

1. **Be positive:** I will search diligently for and acknowledge something good in every person I meet.

2. **Be patient:** I will refuse to get frustrated when others don't do or see things my way.

3. **Be peaceable:** I will avoid unnecessary conflicts, let go of past offenses, and make peace wherever I go.

4. **Be proactive:** I will reach out and take initiative to help others every opportunity I get.

5. **Be polite:** I will show kindness to all I meet, whether they deserve it or not.

6. **Be prayerful:** I will pray for all those who struggle or are in the midst of hard times.

7. **Be protective:** I will stand up and assist those who are being ignored or taken advantage of.

Will you join me?

VERSE TO REMEMBER

There is no greater love than to lay down one's life for one's friends.—JOHN 15:13

QUESTIONS TO PONDER

+ As humans, we tend to give love to people only in the amount and quality they have given us. If they don't give, we don't give. If they give halfheartedly, we give halfheartedly. If they give deeply and richly, so do we. Yet Jesus asked the pointed question, "If you are kind only to your friends, how are you different from anyone else?" (Matthew

5:47). How might you start today to give back in the form of love for those around you?

+ Victor Hugo, author of *Les Misérables*, wrote, "To love another person is to see the face of God." What does that mean, in practical terms?

+ Sometimes giving back requires that we move beyond our comfort zones. When is it most difficult for you to show God's love to others?

QUOTE TO INSPIRE

One word or a pleasing smile is often enough to raise up a saddened and wounded soul.

—SAINT THÉRÈSE OF LISIEUX

I woke up early this morning.

Our bedroom was still in half-shadows, and Tami lay beside me, breathing softly as her golden hair spilled onto the pillow. The windows were open wide, and I could hear the birds celebrating the sunrise—robins, sparrows, blue jays. Even a woodpecker was awake, telegraphing his rapid-fire tap-tap-tapping on the old, rotten snag down by the creek. As I lay there, the words and thoughts and stories of all these previous pages rushed through my head. I pondered my faith and wondered how to put all of this into practice. I told God that it all seems too confusing and hard and scary. *How do I put it all together? How do I figure it all out? How do I live the sort of life that reaches beyond the safety and security and monotony of an ordinary existence?*

Mornings feel magical to me as everything starts to come to life. Sunset frequently holds the same sort of mystery. It's almost as if dawn and dusk provide a thinness in the fabric of nature where God's grace and grandeur can shine through. And if my eyes are open, these are the times when clarity and conviction that seem unarguable capture my heart. Yet this sort of awareness so easily slips away as the full sun of the day's activities blinds me to the supernatural, or the blackness of night draws me into its darkness.

Faith is an odd word. It frequently carries so much meaning that it becomes meaningless. It's like the hundred-year-old bedroom door I once tried to restore. Layer by layer, I stripped and sanded off twelve coats of paint—tan, white, green, brown, pink, and many others I could barely identify. Each color gave the door a different look and represented a different decade.

When I finally got down to the golden oak, I stood in amazement at its beauty. This was not just any door. It was a woodworker's masterpiece. I later learned that the door and the house that held it had been built by a loving father for his son and his new bride as a wedding gift.

Sometimes a door is a lot more than a door. And sometimes faith is a lot more than you ever imagined it to be.

Faith is not a safe thing. It is wild and wonderful. It is often difficult to define and even more difficult to fully understand. I know people who throw words like *faith* and *Christian* and *religion* around like they know exactly what they're talking about. Yet the more they talk, the shallower and more contrived their definitions seem to me. They talk about these words as if they contain nothing supernatural or mysterious or extraordinary. It's like my old door with so many coats of paint that you can't see the texture or grains beneath it all.

Once I strip all the layers of paint off my faith, I realize that authentic faith always involves a risk. Not some small, calculated, comfortable risk, but something big. Faith is neither easy nor comfortable. Oh, it may be easy and comfortable to talk about it. And it's easy to claim you have it or even put other people down for not having it. But ultimately, faith with integrity requires action, and that action requires risk.

But stepping beyond my fears, my selfishness, my comfort zone is something that does not come naturally to me. I am a cautious person. I like everything to be organized and carefully planned before I go on any kind of journey. I want to understand the lay of the land and know the nature of my destination. If there are any risks ahead, I want to know how to avoid or at least minimize them. Yet this is not how faith works. Faith is always a leap in the dark with the hope that you will land somewhere safe. It's believing that even if you are not safe you will at least be falling into the hands, the face, and the providence of God. We might make this leap with reluctance and fear, but when we launch out we'll find it to be the most wonderful, amazing, extraordinary leap any person on this planet could ever take.

So why am I so careful? Why is my heart so willing but my mind so quick to come up with a million reasons why stepping out is not practical or reasonable or wise? If faith is the core of Christian spirituality, then I know that to follow this path I must be willing to throw caution to the wind and risk all.

Pascal, in his famous wager about faith in God, said that we should risk without hesitation because "if you gain, you gain all; if you lose, you lose nothing." I sit in the convenience and comfort of my easy life and agree 100 percent. Yet a risking faith is neither convenient nor comfortable, even though I have everything to gain and nothing to lose.

I know that a life of faith ultimately means letting go. I truly need to step beyond my fears, then step even further. I want to do this, but I hesitate. I hold on and hold back. I yearn for assurance and security, but I am satisfied with neither. To risk involves turning my back on security. As Alberto Hurtado, a Jesuit priest from Chile, wrote, "There is no risk when there is no danger or doubt, anxiety or fear."

Deep inside I want to be like Abraham when he left his homeland to find a new country, or Moses when he left the desert to face the pharaoh, or John and Peter when they left their fishing nets to follow Jesus. An act of faith always involves risk. In fact, without some form of risk taking there can be no faith.

Peter Drucker, the internationally known business guru, defined four types of risk:

1. the risk one must accept
2. the risk one can afford to accept
3. the risk one cannot afford to take
4. the risk one cannot afford not to take

Christian spirituality is this final type of risk. To believe is to risk, and to risk is to leap into God. A risking faith is a willingness to go places you've never gone before, do things you've never done before, face fears you've never faced before, trust God like you've never trusted him before. This type of risk takes you to discovery and to adventure and to excitement and ultimately to God.

My friend Jerry called me today to let me know he was in town. Jerry, the monk–social worker–bounty hunter–private investigator–nuclear power site analyst–seminary administrator–philosopher–writer, is a vagabond who has more adventures on his résumé than a centipede has legs.

For a full ten years Jerry and our good friend Rick, the actor-artist-videographer, and I were inseparable. But that was a long time ago, when we were in our twenties and college students. We were "footloose and fancy-free," as the old saying goes. Together we went to movies, played basketball, hung out at Powell's Bookstore, visited churches, and spent countless evenings at Magellan's Pub. But mostly we just talked. We talked for hours and hours about art and philosophy, the great writers and the meaning of life, politics and religion—the topics were endless.

But then Rick and I settled down. We found steady jobs and got married and had kids. Meanwhile Jerry went off on another of his many adventures. In the midst of the hectic pace and responsibilities of life we lost contact with each other.

Now, some twenty years later, Jerry, Rick, and I found ourselves sitting in my backyard talking about our journeys and where we are in life. The sun was setting and a thunderstorm was flashing its lightning all around us. But we didn't care. We were simply lost in conversation.

"Let's go on an adventure together," Jerry enthusiastically suggested.

"What if the three of us went on a pilgrimage to the Holy Land?" I asked as I got caught up in the moment.

Rick stroked his long, gray beard and said nothing.

"I know one of the bishops in Jerusalem," Jerry said excitedly. "And there are some great monasteries in Greece and Turkey if we wanted to take some side trips."

"What about planning something for a year from this fall?" I said, still needing to include a *little* bit of structure.

"We can do this!" Jerry proclaimed.

Rick nodded his head with a sparkle in his eye.

"Then it's a deal," I said.

For some, our pilgrimage might seem like a small, somewhat insignificant risk. For others, it might seem like no risk at all. But for me it feels like a big risk. I'm excited but anxious. I know this journey with these old friends will take me into the mysterious and unknown, beyond my comfort zone and deep into the unfamiliar. It will also take me into the heart of God, forcing me to dive into him. It may be just a little step, but for me this is risking faith.

That night as I lay on my bed, I dreamed of three middle-aged pilgrims walking the dusty, sunbaked streets of Jerusalem. We walked the ways of Jesus and pondered his words: "If any of you wants to be my follower, you must turn from your selfish ways, take up your cross, and follow me" (Matthew 16:24). Even in my dreams, my mind was reeling.

+ Is it safe?
+ Is it comfortable?
+ Does any of this make any sense?
+ Do I really want to do this?

In my dream I saw Jerry laughing and saying, "Don't worry. Take a risk."

"But are you sure?" Rick and I asked.

Jerry smiled. "The greater the danger, the greater the risk. And therefore the greater the faith and the greater the benefits."

As I awake, I think about the last scene of my dream. Three travelers, earnestly pursuing a risking faith, look high onto a hill above the city—a hill called Golgotha, a hill with three lonely crosses. Then the three of us slip on simple canvas backpacks, and without looking back we say, "Let's go."

Aelred of Rievaulx. *Spiritual Friendship*. Cistercian Publications.

Albom, Mitch. *Tuesdays with Morrie*. Doubleday.

Allender, Dan. *The Healing Path*. Waterbrook.

Arends, Carolyn. *Living the Questions*. Harvest House.

Augustine. *Confessions*. Fine Editions Press.

Barton, Ruth. *Invitation to Solitude and Silence*. InterVarsity.

Benner, David. *Sacred Companions*. InterVarsity.

Benson, Robert. *Between the Dreaming and the Coming True*. Tarcher.

Bernard of Clairvaux. *The Steps of Humility and Pride*. Cistercian Publications.

Bjorklund, Lynda Hunter. *The Hungry Heart*. Tyndale.

Bonhoeffer, Dietrich. *Life Together*. HarperSanFrancisco.

Buchanan, Mark. *Things Unseen*. Multnomah.

Bunyan, John. *The Pilgrim's Progress*. Oxford University Press.

Card, Michael. *A Violent Grace*. Multnomah.

Carmichael, Amy. *Whispers of His Power*. Bethany.

Carroll, Lewis. *Through the Looking-Glass and What Alice Found There*. Signet Classics.

Chambers, Oswald. *My Utmost for His Highest*. Discovery House.

Chesterton, G. K. *Orthodoxy*. BiblioBazaar.

Colson, Charles. *Loving God*. Zondervan.

Cymbala, Jim. *The Life God Blesses*. Zondervan.

Dekker, Ted. *The Slumber of Christianity*. Thomas Nelson.

Dickinson, Emily. *Collected Poems*. Gramercy.

Dillard, Annie. *For the Time Being*. Knopf.

Dillard, Annie. *Teaching a Stone to Talk*. Harper & Row.

Edwards, Jonathan. *The Religious Affections*. Sovereign Grace Publishers.

Eliot, T. S. *The Complete Poems and Plays*. Harcourt.

Elliott, Bill. *Falling into the Face of God*. Thomas Nelson.

Fénelon, François. *Christian Perfection*. Bethany.

Foster, Richard. *Celebration of Discipline*. Harper & Row.

Francis de Sales. *Introduction to the Devout Life*. Vintage.

Fromm, Erich. *The Art of Loving*. Harper.

Gire, Ken. *The Reflective Life*. Chariot Victor.

Guinness, Os. *The Call*. Thomas Nelson.

Hanegraaff, Hank. *The Prayer of Jesus*. Word.

Hershey, Terry. *Sacred Necessities*. Sorin Books.

Hugo, Victor. *Les Misérables*. Signet Classics.

Ignatius of Loyola. *Spiritual Exercises*. Kessinger Publishing.

Ingram, Chip. *God as He Really Is*. Baker.

James, Steven. *Sailing Between the Stars*. Revell.

John of the Cross. *Ascent of Mount Carmel*. Cosimo Classics.

John of the Cross. *Dark Night of the Soul*. Dover.

Johnson, Ben Campbell. *The God Who Speaks*. Eerdmans.

Julian of Norwich. *Revelations of Divine Love*. Penguin Classics.

Kafka, Franz. *The Trial*. Schocken Books.

Keller, Helen. *Light in My Darkness*. Chrysalis Books.

Kelly, Thomas. *A Testament of Devotion.* HarperSanFrancisco.

Kempis, Thomas à. *The Imitation of Christ.* Ava Maria Press.

Kierkegaard, Søren. *Purity of Heart.* Harper.

Kreeft, Peter. *Everything You Ever Wanted to Know about Heaven.* Ingatius Press.

Ledbetter, J. Otis. *In the Secret Place.* Multnomah.

Lewis, C. S. *Mere Christianity.* Macmillan.

Lewis, C. S. *The Weight of Glory.* Eerdmans.

MacDonald, George. *The Diary of an Old Soul.* BiblioBazaar.

Manning, Brennan. *The Rabbi's Heartbeat.* NavPress.

Manning, Brennan. *The Ragamuffin Gospel.* Multnomah.

McManus, Erwin. *Seizing Your Divine Moment.* Thomas Nelson.

Meeder, Kim. *Hope Rising.* Multnomah.

Merton, Thomas. *New Seeds of Contemplation.* New Directions.

Miller, Calvin. *The Table of Inwardness.* InterVarsity.

Miller, Donald. *Blue Like Jazz.* Thomas Nelson.

Mother Teresa of Calcutta. *A Simple Path.* Ballantine Books.

Mulholland, Robert. *Invitation to a Journey.* InterVarsity.

Müller, George. *Answers to Prayer.* Moody.

Nee, Watchman. *The Normal Christian Life.* Hendrickson.

Needham, David. *Close to His Majesty.* Multnomah.

Nicholas of Cusa. *Selected Spiritual Writings.* Paulist Press.

Norris, Kathleen. *Amazing Grace: A Vocabulary of Faith.* Riverhead Books.

Nouwen, Henri. *Life of Beloved*. Crossroad.

Nouwen, Henri. *The Way of the Heart*. HarperSanFrancisco.

Ortberg, John. *God Is Closer than You Think*. Zondervan.

Packer, J. I. *Knowing God*. InterVarsity.

Pascal, Blaise. *Pensées*. Penguin Classics.

Peale, Norman Vincent. *The Power of Positive Thinking*. Running Press.

Peterson, Eugene. *Leap Over a Wall*. HarperSanFrancisco.

Pippert, Rebecca Manley. *Hope Has Its Reasons*. InterVarsity.

Pope John Paul II. *The Way to Christ*. HarperOne.

Ramsey, Michael. *Be Still and Know*. Cowley Publications.

Raybon, Patricia. *I Told the Mountain to Move*. Tyndale.

Reeve, Pamela. *Deserts of the Heart*. Multnomah.

Sayers, Dorothy. *The Mind of the Maker*. HarperOne.

Schaeffer, Francis. *True Spirituality*. Tyndale.

Shaw, Luci. *The Crime of Living Cautiously*. InterVarsity.

Simpson, A. B. *Seeing the Invisible*. Christian Publications.

Smith, Hannah Whitall. *The Christian's Secret of a Happy Life*. Ballantine Books.

Solzhenitsyn, Aleksandr. *The Gulag Archipelago*. Harper.

Sproul, R. C. *The Holiness of God*. Tyndale.

Spurgeon, Charles. *All of Grace*. Moody.

Stowell, Joseph. *Simply Jesus*. Multnomah.

Swartz, David. *Embracing God*. Harvest House.

Sweet, Leonard. *Carpe Mañana*. Zondervan.

Sweet, Leonard. *Soul Tsunami*. Zondervan.

Swindoll, Charles. *For Those Who Hurt*. Zondervan.

Swindoll, Charles. *Intimacy with the Almighty*. Countryman.

Tenney, Tommy. *The God Catchers*. Thomas Nelson.

Teresa of Avila. *The Interior Castle*. Image.

Teykl, Terry. *The Presence Based Church*. Prayer Point Press.

Thérèse of Lisieux. *The Little Way for Every Day*. Paulist Press.

Thielicke, Helmut. *Notes from a Wayfarer*. Paragon.

Thomas, Gary. *Sacred Pathways*. Zondervan.

Thomas, Gary. *Seeking the Face of God*. Harvest House.

Tolkien, J. R. R. *The Lord of the Rings*. Houghton Mifflin.

Tournier, Paul. *The Meaning of Persons*. Buccaneer.

Tozer, A. W. *The Knowledge of the Holy*. Christian Publications.

Tozer, A. W. *The Pursuit of God*. Christian Publications.

Warne, Joel. *The Intimate Journey*. Wellspring.

Warren, Rick. *The Purpose-Driven Life*. Zondervan.

West, Jessamyn. *The Quaker Reader*. Pendle Hill.

White, James Emery. *Embracing the Mysterious God*. InterVarsity.

Wiersbe, Warren. *A Gallery of Grace*. Kregel.

Willard, Dallas. *The Divine Conspiracy*. HarperSanFrancisco.

Yancey, Philip. *Reaching for the Invisible God*. Zondervan.

Zacharias, Ravi. *Cries of the Heart*. Thomas Nelson.

OTHER BOOKS BY DR. STEVE STEPHENS

20 (Surprisingly Simple) Rules and Tools for a Great Marriage

20 (Surprisingly Simple) Rules and Tools for a Great Family

20 (Surprisingly Simple) Rules and Tools for a Great Day

Blueprints for a Solid Marriage

The Worn Out Woman

The Walk Out Woman

The Wounded Woman

The Wounded Warrior

Lost in Translation

ACKNOWLEDGMENTS

Tami, who walks beside me.

Keely, who inputs all my scribbles.

Lisa, who edits like a master.

David, who is a great cheerleader.

John, who believed in me from the beginning.

Jan, who gave this book a chance.

Sharon, Doug, Sarah, Stephanie, and all the other incredible people at Tyndale.

The many teachers, mentors, and friends who have encouraged me in this spiritual journey.

ABOUT THE AUTHOR

DR. STEVE STEPHENS is a psychologist, Sunday school teacher, storyteller, seminar speaker, and author of some twenty books with more than a million copies sold. But most important, he seeks to follow God, be a good husband, love his three wonderful children, and live a decent, compassionate, meaningful life.

In his free time, Steve has squeezed in being a youth pastor, a radio talk show host, a guest professor, a president of a community marriage policy committee, and a board member on various Christian ministries.

Steve has a master's degree in pastoral psychology and a doctorate in counseling/clinical psychology from Western Seminary and George Fox University.

Steve and his wife, Tami, have been married for twenty-four years and live on an acre and a half of gardens in Happy Valley, Oregon. They love to laugh, read, garden, hike, explore, barbecue, visit friends, and have fun with their three children—Brittany, Dylan, and Dusty. They also like to escape to Mexico, Hawaii, or the Caribbean any chance they get.

ALSO AVAILABLE BY DR. STEVE STEPHENS

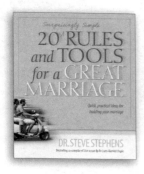 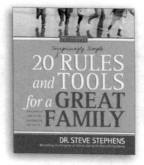 

If you want your life to be simply great, you'll be amazed at the impact a few simple steps can make. Each book offers twenty clear, to-the-point principles to keep your marriage, your family, and your self strong and vibrant. Each chapter includes a prayer to strengthen your relationships and concrete ideas to help you enjoy life as never before.

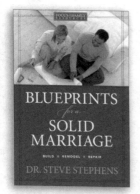

A marriage, like a house, requires time, effort, and regular maintenance. Whether you're in need of light remodeling, minor repairs, or major reconstruction, *Blueprints for a Solid Marriage* offers more than fifty practical projects that will help you quickly assess and enhance your relationship and lay the foundation for marital bliss.